Tracy,
I pray story a[...] [mini]sters to your spirit as only God can do. Please take your time and go through a journey

from Ashes to Beauty

(an autobiography)

of heartbreaks but God has healed and delivered me in many areas and only He can do it. There is nothing to hard for God. God bless you and keep

Raw. Real. Relatable.

you. Love,

Dana Delores Meeks

Copyright 2020 Raw. Real. Relatable.
All rights reserved. No part of this publication may be reproduced, stored in a retrieval system, or transmitted, in any form or by any means, electronic, mechanical, photocopying, recording, or otherwise, without the prior written permission of the author. Printed in the United States of America.

Book Disclaimer
All names used are fictitious for privacy purposes. Some content and language may be explicit.

Cover design by Chauncey Flowers

Raw. Real. Relatable. 2020

First Edition Published December 2020

ISBN 978-0-578-23949-1

Chapters

Chapter One..........................Setting the Stage
Chapter Two...............Seeing the Real Picture
Chapter Three..................Falling on Hard Times
Chapter Four....................Growing Up Too Fast
Chapter Five......................... Secrets Revealed
Chapter Six...............Living a Lifestyle of Lies
Chapter Seven................Pandora's Box Opens
Chapter Eight.............................Falling Apart
Chapter Nine.....................Turmoil to Tragedy
Chapter Ten..................................Devastation
Chapter Eleven.........What are You Saying God?
Chapter Twelve......Trying to Make Sense of It All
Chapter Thirteen...............................Transition
Chapter Fourteen............A Blessing and A Curse
Chapter Fifteen.............................It Got Worse
Chapter Sixteen.................Picking Up the Pieces
Chapter Seventeen...............Self-Discovery Mode

Foreword
But He said to me, "My grace is sufficient for you, for my power is made perfect in weakness." Therefore, I will boast all the more gladly of my weaknesses, so that the power of Christ may rest upon me. For the sake of Christ, then, I am content with weaknesses, insults, hardships, persecutions, and calamities. For when I am weak, then I am strong.
2 Corinthians 12:9-10

The bible is so clear in this scripture, and although we face so many things in life, we should not forget the word of God. When I met Dana Meeks and her daughter at a church we were attending in October 2000. We both were single parents and attended some of the same ministry events. We instantly became friends.

The more time we spent together Dana felt comfortable enough to share her story. I was surprised that one person could endurance so many trials in their young life. In this book Dana will share her ups and downs, challenges and triumphs so don't rush through it, take your time because you don't want to miss anything.

Dana has experienced the loss of her mother, suicide of her brother, imprisonment of her father, personal heartaches and heartbreaks. God has kept her close to His heart even while she was going through because He knew the plans, he's had for her. He has allowed me to walk through this journey of her healing with her. She served as my armor bearer and prayer partner in a women's ministry, Sisters in the Spirit Ministry, Inc. which started in 2001 and later a minister at Dominion Life Faith and Worship where my husband Terance is Senior Pastor and I serve as Co-Pastor.

At times, life hasn't been easy for Dana and as you will read in this book that she's not always made the right choices, done or said the right things. However, she like many of us have allowed our experiences to teach us wisdom, understanding and knowledge. She's a fighter in the natural as well as in the spirit. I have to laugh because I can remember times when her delivery of some of her words were just a little salty. LOL.

As her friend, I can say that. You have to know her and to know her heart. Yes, she will definitely tell it like it is but in the same way she will give you the shirt off her back. I've seen God use Dana prophetically, in spiritual warfare and healing. God has isolated her in this season for many reasons, however I believe one of the reasons is that He is strengthening her to do damage to the kingdom of darkness and her experiences will help her to fight harder and more fervently.

Dana has always prayed and understood who God is. There were times she just wanted to do things her way, not necessarily because she felt she knew what was best but because she felt it was easier. In this season of Dana's life, she has been hearing the voice of the Lord clearly and is being obedient to His instructions and directions. We must understand, there are times even in obedience it will not be easy.

God's word never told us that we won't face problems, challenges, situations or sufferings in our life that may even take us off course. Again, the word says in 2 Corinthians 12:9 is that His Grace is sufficient for you, for His power is made perfect in our weakness. During the time of weakness, we have to know and understand who God is. I truly believe that during those time of weaknesses God stepped in and Dana was strengthened and restored.

As you read, allow your hearts and mind to be open. God wants to heal some areas of your life and this book will bring revelation, restoration and healing. Dana knows that even in writing her book she's had to endure many challenges but one thing for sure, she is aware that all things have worked together for her good, because she loves the Lord.

And we know that for those who love God all things work together for good, for those who are called according to His purpose.
Romans 8:28

Debra Reddick, Co-Pastor
Dominion Life Faith and Worship Church, Tampa, Florida
Debra Reddick Ministries, Founder

Introduction

This autobiography has been written to encourage and empower all that have experienced trauma. It has been inspired by real life events and directed by the leading and guiding of the Holy Spirit, to share my testimony and life's struggles depicted in an authentic timeline of occurrences.

My goal is to take you on a journey of abandonment, anger issues, confusion, depression, displacement, frustrations, and rejection. I have experienced several traumatic events and want to share God's Faith, Hope and Love that has sustained me until this very moment.

I only had my parents for 19 years and lost them in an instance and never recovered a mother or father figure. I had no mother-figure to mentor me from a young lady to womanhood. No real representation of love from a man including my dad. My discovery of learning to love God, myself and others has been a necessity, to gaining and keeping my peace, to triumph over the devil and his schemes, as well as overcome life's trials, which is a continual process.

I understand millions may not have had parents from birth and much younger, therefore my heart sincerely goes out to you.

But without faith it is impossible to please him for he that cometh to God must believe that He is, a rewarder of them that diligently seek Him Hebrews 11:6 (KJV)

Then the Lord answered me and said: "Write the vision and make it plain on tablets, that he may run who reads it. For the vision is yet for an appointed time; But at the end it will speak, and it will not lie. Though it tarries, wait for it; Because it will surely come, it will not tarry. "Behold the proud, His soul is not upright in him; But the just shall live by his faith. Habakkuk 2:2-4 (NKJV)

For I know the thoughts that I think toward you, saith the Lord, thoughts of peace, and not of evil, to give you an expected end. Jeremiah 29:11 (KJV)

Chapter one
Setting the Stage

My mom was born in Twin, Lakes Florida. She was number 8 of 9 children and the youngest girl from my grandparents. She got all the hand-me-downs from her older sisters. My grandparents were sharecroppers as well as entrepreneurs. My granddaddy (jovial and talkative) ran his own a BBQ pit and juke joint and my grandmother was a Pentecostal minister (serious and stern) who sold Avon and Old 97 products. They were also fishermen. During different times of the year, they travelled to different states picking the crop that was in season. Neither of my maternal grandparents were the affectionate type.

My dad was born in Lake City, Florida. He was raised in the house with his dad and younger brother and was the oldest of 5. As I have been told my paternal grandmother passed on the day I was born, therefore I never had the pleasure of meeting her. My parents grew up in a small town called Lacoochee, Florida in humble beginnings. They grew up closely together, almost like family because they lived near one another from childhood and my mom has siblings my dad's age and older. My grandparents helped raise him. One of my mom's older sisters and my dad were in the same class and one of her older brothers went into the military at the same time with him. My dad was 4 years older than my mom and always took care of her financially. When he completed high school, he took his diploma and missed his commencement ceremony and enlisted in the US Air Force in 1963. My mom was finishing the 8th grade. He did a lot for her and whatever he could for both of their families. He certainly had a lot on his plate for a young man. Once my mom graduated from high school in 1967, she went off to college on a full academic scholarship to Allen University, a HBCU in Columbia, South Carolina with a couple of her friends from her small town of Lacoochee. My dad had given her credit cards, money and access for whatever she wanted. Therefore, she was ballin' in school. My dad served a short term of 3 years in the Air Force escaping going to the Vietnam war. After my mom's Freshman year in college, she returned home. My parents got married in December 1968 and I was born December 1969, at 7 months premature weighing a whole 4 pounds 0 ounces at Memorial Hospital in Dade City, Florida.

  I am the oldest of 2 children that my parents had together. However, growing up I was the only child for a while. I grew up with the maternal side of our families and did not get to know the paternal side until I was grown. However, I grew up around my paternal granddaddy Meeks with his last wife. I stayed with them on some weekends and during the summertime. My granddaddy was well off and always drove a new vehicle. He had land, livestock, and crops that he sold. I remember as a little girl waking up early mornings and going outside with him to feed the animals. I absolutely loved my granddaddy, and he was crazy about me! He gave me everything, especially money. He had money and land for me that was fraudulently changed after he died so I never got anything. He passed when I was in the 11th grade. Unfortunately, I witnessed him being mean and verbally abusive to his wife at times, but I could not understand why because she was a girl like me from a child's perspective. He had anger issues and was married 3 to 4 times.

  We lived in the Lacoochee and Dade City area until I was 2 years old, then my parents moved to Tampa, which is 45 minutes South of Dade City. Tampa was considered the big city from where they hailed from. They purchased a new mobile home, which was happening back then, but their relationship suffered and was unfavorable due to my dad's continued abuse to my mom, and his addiction to alcohol and gambling. Almost 2 years after moving to Tampa, they separated. They sold their mobile home and my dad enlisted in the US Army in 1973.

  Once my dad left, we moved to Ponce De Leon housing projects. I was almost 4 years old and the kids there were terrible. Baby, I was in for a rude awakening and had to learn real quick, to get in where I fit in. I can remember getting into fights when I went outside to play. The kids were jealous of me because I had long hair, wore nice clothes and shoes, had toys, or whatever! This is where my mischievous and rebellious personality kicked in because I gave them hell back! After a short time, I met a nice girl my age that lived straight across from us and she lived with her mom and older brother. We became best friends and so did our moms. We went everywhere together, even when my dad came home to visit us on leave. She would go on vacations with us to theme parks. Fun times!

> **"When someone shows you who they are, believe them the first time."**
> **-Maya Angelou**

Chapter Two

Seeing the Real Picture

My mom was pretty, slender, nicely figured, well-dressed, a class act and soft-spoken. She did not cuss, drink alcohol or smoke, who worked as a secretary during the day and her hobby at night was bowling, which she did year-round. She also loved to dance, sew, and volunteer in community activities and events in Tampa. She was also a member of National Council of Negro Women and well-known. Lorene was her name, but she went by Terry which was her nickname. I remember her having male friends that would come over periodically but the main one was Jorge, a handsome Puerto Rican gentleman, dark-skinned, well dressed in suits most times with a full beard, who was very kind to us. He was the closest person like a father-figure during my childhood years, but he was also married. I remember going to his aunt's house who lived in Robles Park another housing project not far from us and they would feed us great Spanish foods and desserts, to this day Spanish food is one of my favorites. My mom enjoyed drinking Café Con Leche with them. Jorge's younger brother and some of his family knew about us and his relationship with my mom. He had 2 sons who were close to my age with his wife that he would bring over as well.

We ended up moving out of the projects after living there maybe 2 years and moved into a predominantly white neighborhood at the time named Del Rio Estates, when I was close to 5 years old. This is where the foundation of my childhood started from ages 5 to 13 years old. My dad really didn't have many conversations with me or teach me on much of anything, so I was thankful to have Jorge in my life because he talked to me about boys and how to conduct myself as a young lady around boys, and how boys should treat and respect me. I absolutely adored Jorge and believe this is when I became obsessed with men with beards from a little girl.

SN: Pay attention to your likes and dislikes as you journey through life, to see where your issues (positive or negative) stem from?

I recall riding in the back seat of the car while an older White man, who was the realtor driving around showing my mom homes in the Black neighborhoods in East Tampa. Nevertheless, my mom kept telling him that she wanted to see homes in the Del Rio Estates area, better known as The Fishbowl, and all the streets were named after fish or marine life. My parents purchased a home, and my dad used his military benefits to assist in the purchase.

We moved into a 3/2 home with a single-car garage with a nice front yard and backyard. If I recall correctly, we were the first Blacks on Perch Street in 1975. My new elementary school was literally around the corner, so I walked to school.

I was a Latch-key kid because my mom was a single-parent who worked Monday through Friday 7:00am to 4:00pm. I got home around 2:30pm from school, so I was not home very long before my mom got home. She forbade me to go outside or have anyone in the house and do not touch the stove! I would from time to time, but her 6th sense would kick in and she always knew, and I would get into trouble. The kids on my street and in the neighborhood were more friendly than those bad ass kids in the projects, but there were more boys than girls to play with.

However, I still found enjoyment in playing with them in kickball, touch football, and freeze-tag. We climbed trees, raced in the street, rode our bicycles and I had a skateboard too. I continued getting into fights from time to time because the boys would try me by pulling my hair or feeling on my butt and running off, but I would hawk them down and fight them.

My mom was a young mom (had me at 20) who went out often on the weekends with her male friends. I was home alone most of the times. Whenever she got a babysitter for me, I would run them off! I preferred to be by myself. Just grown! My dad would come home on leave once or twice a year for approximately 15 to 30 days to visit us on his leave. When he did, they would have card parties and get-togethers with their old friends from Lacoochee/Dade City. I remember one night they had friends over who had a son and daughter close to my age. We were in the den playing and the son pushed me, and I hit the corner of my table set and pulled the skin off my stomach, which bled a little. I went to tell on him, and my dad brushed it off and said I would be alright. Well, that was not the response I was looking for, so I picked up my chair to the table and hit him in the face with it and knocked his tooth out! There was so much commotion around it that my dad beat me for the first time in my life at 6 years old.

At 10 years old, my parents reconciled and decided to live under the same roof again. My dad was stationed at Fort Benning, Georgia. I was in the 5th grade and we lived on post. It was a difficult adjustment for me because I had to ride the bus for the first time and I didn't like it or the kids because they were corny, and my teacher was mean. I ended up having my mom talk to my teacher because she was rude as hell! This move was an eye-opener for me because I realized that my dad was an alcoholic, had anger issues, and was abusing my mom emotionally, verbally and most of all physically. Apparently, my mom was hiding this information because she later told me that my dad had been beating her since she was pregnant with me, hence that was the main reason they separated when I was 2 years old. I was always awakened out of my sleep at night to my dad's loud antics and my mom screaming in agony, pleading with him to stop, or calling out my name to help her. She was being pushed down the stairs in the house, being straddled by him while lying on her back in the bed, being punched repeatedly until she was black and blue with bruises all over face and body. I remember a time that I was awakened and went downstairs to the living room where they were and my mom was crying because my dad was twisting her arm behind her to the point that it could break. I had to go up to him and insist that he stop! He was telling me to go back to bed and I said not until you let my mom go! I waited on her and we went back upstairs to my room together. Another time that I was awakened out of my sleep to chaos, I opened their bedroom door, and he was straddled over her punching her like a boxing bag. I yelled at him to release her and he yelled for me to go back in my room. I said absolutely not, and if he did not let her go, I was calling the MP's (Military Police). He released her and I waited for my mom to get up and go into the bathroom to clean herself up, then we went into my bedroom and I closed the door. I was always put in the position to intervene and question my dad for his behavior. When I questioned him, he would always stop because he did not want me to witness his tirades. I vividly recall telling my mom that this had to stop and if not, I would kill him! She told me not to say that and I replied, I mean it! She said that she would get us out of this mess. I prayed out loud for us and we went to sleep. My dad never said another word nor did he touch my door that night. What is it for a 10-year old to have such responsibility? I was never afraid of my dad or anyone for that matter. A fearless kid I was! Early the next morning, he left for PT (Physical Training) and work as usual and my mom made me go to school because I wanted to stay home and protect her from him. When I got home from school, she told me that we were moving back home soon. While I was at school my mom had spoken to her parents, and her oldest sister to inform them of what was going on and it had gotten worse, I guess me telling her that I would kill my dad was a wake-up call for her. Sad truth! You would think that a person would want the best for themselves before anyone else.

My mom went to the doctor shortly after that incident for her well woman exam and found out that she was pregnant. Now this is the second time pregnant and being abused. She told me but did not tell my dad while we were still in the house with him. My mom packed a suitcase and a bag and hid them in my bedroom closet, within that same week we left on the Greyhound bus headed back to Tampa, while my dad was working. In a week, we were back there with my granddaddy (mom's dad), my godfather, my uncle (mom's older brother) and my aunt (mom's oldest sister). We loaded up in my grandmother's van and went back to Fort Benning late one night to get our furniture and car. Once we arrived, it was daybreak and we had to wait until U-Haul opened to get a truck. My godfather actually drove trucks for a living, so he drove the U-Haul. The men loaded all the heavy furniture, and the women carried all the light things (my mom pregnant), while my dad was at work. Before the loading was completed, we saw my dad across the field peeking at us to see what was going on, but he never came over to the house. What a coward! However, my dad was shy and very introverted. He never wanted anyone to know his business and definitely not family members.

The LORD is good, A stronghold in the day of trouble; And He knows those who trust in Him. Nahum 1:7 (NKJV)

Chapter Three

Falling on Hard Times

When we got back to Tampa, there was a tenant still leasing our house because the lease was for a year and we came back from Georgia in less than 6 months. My mom had to get an apartment with a 7-month lease, about 15 minutes from my old elementary school. I had to go to school, but we didn't have transportation because our car was having mechanical issues, so she asked my godparents if I could stay with them until she got her vehicle back on the road. They agreed and I stayed with them during the week for a couple of months, but I went home on the weekends because my mom was showing in her pregnancy and needed my assistance. She and my dad continued having challenges, my dad was grudgeful that we left and also because he was ashamed that the family knew what was going on. The argument now was him asking if she was pregnant from him? I knew of her male friends, but I was not aware of any in Georgia.

Unfortunately, he was resentful and refused to send her his monthly allotment and continued to accuse her of cheating and doubting that she was pregnant from him.

My mom kept assuring him that she got pregnant the short time we were in Georgia with him. Due to the lack of his support, she had to get assistance and received Food Stamps (the colored paper coupons) and WIC. I was so embarrassed to go to the store for her with those Food Stamps. She would say, girl I have worked all my life to pay into the system, to get this much needed temporary help. She ended up getting our car fixed and things improved a little. The most memorable times of this period for me was Friday night seafood. We would have a variety of fish, crabs, shrimp and lobster. The crab boils were the bomb! My mom absolutely loved seafood as well as going fishing. She said it was relaxation for her and I hated going...Boring!

My mom gave birth to my little brother on July 13, 1980. One my childhood friend's mom took her to the hospital. She drove fast and she was funny as hell! That ride was hilarious! My dad did not come to Florida from Georgia, but my mom did inform him that she was in labor. My life forever changed because I was no longer the only child.

At times, I was angry that my mom got pregnant, but once I saw my baby brother, I embraced having him around and he quickly became my favorite person. I was like his other mom because I always wanted to care for him, to allow my mom to have a break, so I babysat him without her asking me. We finally moved back into our house on Perch street while my brother was still an infant.

This was a very trying time for my parent's marriage. Before long, my dad had taken leave and came home to see his son, for the first time, whom, was born the day after his July 12th birthday.

He shall deliver you in six troubles, Yes, in seven no evil shall touch you. Job 5:19 (NKJV)

Chapter Four
Growing up Too Fast

My dad was still trippin' with his financial support, so my mom started working at a daycare center across the street from my elementary school, so I walked over after school each day. Fortunately, she was handling all the struggles as best as she could. I knew it was hard on her, so I helped her out with whatever she needed without her asking. I was very clean, organized and disciplined from a kid. Now as an adult I am OCD, not extreme but some may disagree with me. LOL!

Jorge was coming back over to the house like we never left. I am sure they loved one another. I paid attention to them, but somehow never really questioned the series of events that transpired. The old school mentality in Black households...whatever goes on in the house stays in the house... also, do what I say and not as I do. This way of thinking has kept millions in bondage to this day. I was a kid, so I did what I was told and now that I am grown, I have had to recover from those dysfunctional ideologies. I was a pretty good kid in elementary school, the only trouble I would get into was from being a class-clown. I would complete my work early and be disruptive from laughing and playing. My teacher had to visit my house 2 or 3 times for my behavior.

When I was not at home, I would be with my god sister at their house or at the neighborhood park, Nuccio. My god sister was loud and wild, and my mom disliked her influence on me. She certainly was not a good role model, but I did everything she did because I looked up to her, but why did I do that? I honestly cannot explain it to this very day because I was the one that had everything going for me. She was 2 years older than me and the youngest of her 4 siblings, Eddie and Kevin older brothers and Evette. Our parents worked at the same job. My mom was one of the secretaries at a chemical plant and her dad was a truck driver. They became friends and we were introduced to his family.

He and his wife agreed to be my godparents, hence the reason I stayed with them and I spent the night regularly. However, there were some very disturbing things happening to me at their house. My god sisters, Evette and Pamela shared a bedroom with twin beds, and I would sleep in the twin bed with Pamela most of the times or on a palette on the floor in the living room. The oldest brother was molesting me, in the same room, in the same bed with her. He would come in the room and tap on me or shake me until I woke up. I was under 11 years old and it happened for years while staying in that house. He told me I better not tell anyone! Fucking pervert!

SN: I never told my parents. I also did not tell any of my extended family members or any of my friends until my 30's. Abuse in any form has lasting effects on the individual, most are repressed.

The weekend before Thanksgiving every year was The Florida Classics in Tampa, Florida A&M University and Bethune Cookman College, 2 HBCU rivals playing a football game and the city would be jumpin' with excitement and activities. My mom had gone out with her friends and I was home with my little brother, 2 cousins who were sisters, and my god sister. My god sister, Pamela came up with this bright idea in her head and suggested to call some boys over to the house. We called some homeboys that lived near, who we saw almost every day at Nuccio park.

Carl, Antonio, and Larry were brothers and Paul, and Derrick were brothers. Well the shenanigans began, but my 2 cousins did not take part in any part of the foolishness and went into the den with my little brother to watch television. I had sex with Carl the oldest of all the boys and was scared to death. I lost my virginity that night due to peer pressure and was terrified! I was 11 years old turning 12 the next month in December. My first experience having sex was a one-night stand because I had nothing to do with him again and barely spoke if I saw him. My god sister was in another room having sex with Antonio the brother right next to Carl in age. Then when I was coming out the room in disbelief of what I had done, she went into the room and had sex with Carl the same brother I did. She had sex with 2 brothers in the same night and it was her first time too from what she told me. One of the other boys approached me and I said hell no! It was a hoe-asis that night...Ridiculous!

  Antonio (4 years older) and I were like brother and sister. He has known me since I was 5 years old. We were very close and talked almost every day, but Pamela was obsessed with him. Well a few months later, Paul and I started dating for like 3 months and Pamela was talking to Antonio, but nothing serious. He has always denied dating her. My house was the hangout house to have sex because my mom was always gone bowling or on dates. Paul and Pamela realized that Antonio and I had mad chemistry and liked one another. I broke up with Paul and told Antonio how I felt about him, at 13 years old in the 8th grade, we were in a full relationship. The younger brother of Antonio, Larry was dating 2 of my friends and they discovered it. One day while I was at track practice, they called my house and told my mom that pregnant. Females are a trip! When I got home, my mom asked me about it, and I said that I didn't know for sure. She asked was I having sex and I said yes.

  She said that she wanted to speak to his mother and made me dial his phone number. She spoke to his mother and asked to come over to have a conversation in person. The next day we went over to their house and I put the word out for Antonio not to be at home. My mom told her that her son was too old, 17 years old and in the 12th grade, and having sex with her daughter. If I were pregnant, she was making me have an abortion and she was paying half of the cost and they would pay the other half. This lady was a devout Christian and my mom was telling this lady what she was going to pay for. She said, I was going to take a pregnancy test and she would let her know the results and if she saw her son around me or her house again, she was calling the police. When we got home, she beat my ass! I took a home pregnancy test it was positive, so she took me on base to the doctor and it was negative twice. When we got home, she beat my ass again! After that no more staying home alone for me, but I was still sneaking to call Antonio and see him.

So I will restore to you the years that the swarming locust has eaten, The crawling locust,

The consuming locust,

And the chewing locust,

My great army which I sent among you. You shall eat in plenty and be satisfied,

And praise the name of the Lord your God, Who has dealt wondrously with you;

And my people shall never be put to shame.

Joel 2:25-26 (NKJV)

Chapter Five
Secrets Revealed

My parents were getting along better and at least having more communication. When I finished 8th grade in June 1983, my mom told me we were going to Germany to visit my dad for the summer. My dad was stationed in Kitzingen, Germany living in the barracks on post, but had to find somewhere for us to stay. We ended up staying on the economy in a German neighborhood. I was very upset because I did not want to leave Antonio, my boyfriend in Florida. I went into rebellion mode and was sneaking to call him long distance back to the US and running up our phone bill and never said a word. I became very depressed and did not want to go anywhere and stayed in my room all the time listening to old school R&B like The Isley Brothers, Con Funk Shun, Otis Redding, Luther Vandross and The O'Jays and missing Antonio. I was young but an old soul. My parents came up with another bright idea to go on a family vacation, we went to Florence and Rome, Italy, Innsbruck and Vienna, Austria. I wasn't being a brat because I realized how blessed we were to travel to other countries because many people have not left their hometown or state let alone going to other countries. My brother was the celebrity and main attraction on our vacation because everyone was captivated by his complexion, handsome face, and big curly hair. We were gone for 2 weeks, once we returned home, we all were outside cleaning the car and my mom, and I got into a physical altercation. I was still heated and she was getting on my nerves! I reached to get a bottle of cleaner from her and she snatched it saying that I didn't ask for it and I swung on her. She grabbed my shirt and had me pinned, to the point where I could not move, so my dad had to break us up. He demanded that she let me go! About a week after coming back from vacation, my mom dropped the news on me that she wanted to stay with my dad because he was having a difficult time being away from us. She had made a commitment to work on their marriage, which may have been partly true, but I found out they were trying to keep me away from Antonio.

My dad was an introvert, workaholic, and gambled. Our house was the turn-up house because my mom always cooked a lot of great dishes and barbequed and my dad always had the libations on deck, so he would invite his soldiers over to play Dominos, Spades, or Bid Whiz, occasionally Backgammon. It was always loud with music and trash talking from the table of men playing the games. My dad could never drink socially and would always get drunk and belligerent. He would say really mean and antagonizing things to my mom in front of our company, but no one would say anything because he was their superior. A fucking coward! She would be so embarrassed, but it made everyone else feel awkward, so they would leave. Then the bullshit started with the loud talking and name calling! I would always be in my bedroom and would come downstairs to see what was going on. My dad would always yell for me to go back in my room and he would be beating her up. I would scream at him to stop or I would call the authorities on him. He always stopped!

School started and I was 14 years old and a freshman in high school.

It was a school for military kids, 6th through 12th grades and it literally was the biggest school I had seen at the time. I was overwhelmed with trying to figure out all of the confusion going on in my house with my parents, missing my boyfriend in Florida, learning a new school, new kids, and new teachers and trying to keep all this shit straight in my head. Remember I could not tell anyone, so I became more depressed. All I would do when I came home from school would be listening to oldies while doing my homework, then eat dinner and stay in my room. I was so miserable that I started calling the US more often calling my boyfriend.

One day I called Pamela and she told me she was pregnant from Antonio. She was a teen at 16 or 17 at the time and he was grown. We got into an argument and I told her that he did not like her, and she was just some free pussy! Scandalous bitch!

After a few months of being in school, I finally met a friend who was bad as hell! She was a White girl that liked Black boys and she literally hated her stepdad, who was in the military also. He was a racist but never said anything to me when I went over their house. She would occasionally skip school and one day I skipped school with her and went downtown Wurzburg, to go shoplifting. We went in one store after another, but I would not take anything. She kept telling me to take something, and due to peer pressure, I finally stole a shirt. I did not need to steal anything because I got everything I needed and wanted from my parents. I asked her how would she explain taking all those clothes home? She said no one would realize anything. What girl?

Well the day I skipped with her, I wrote my own absence letter for the school and forged my dad's signature because my mom's signature was too hard to copy. The school mailed the letter to my address on file. Oh boy! When I came home from basketball practice, my dad asked me about it and I could not respond because I was not going to lie again, so he showed me the letter, for the second time in my life my dad gave me a beaten. I was so devastated because he did not chastise me or my brother, my mom did all that. Guess what? No more beatings for me! My mom ended up finding the shirt that I stole and made me threw it in the trash. My parents were so upset with me but more disappointed than anything and forbade me to continue keeping company with her because those illegal practices, shoplifting and forgery could get me into more trouble than I wanted to deal with down the road. They were both law-abiding citizens and I wanted to be also. We had neighbors next door, a young married couple in their 20's that I would go over and hangout with them. We would eat, drink alcohol, smoke hash, and watch television. The husband was a soldier and his buddies would come over and they would try to talk to me, and he would tell them that my dad was a E-7/SFC (Sergeant First Class) and they got out of my face. I had a boyfriend at school by then and I was not thinking about grown ass men. He and I both played basketball and travelled to games together because the boys and girls rode on the same bus to away games. I was doing what I wanted by this time because I was over my parent's bullshit!

One night, my dad had his soldiers over to the house drinking and playing cards and decided to drive them back to the barracks when they were ready to leave, for whatever reason he did not feel he was drunk. My mom told him that he had too much to drink but he argued her down that he was fine, so he drove them anyway. He ended up getting stopped by the Polizei (German Police). When they recognized they were American soldiers the MP's were called (Military Police) and my dad did a breathalyzer and was cited a DUI and taken to jail, actually holding cell. A huge mess and ordeal it was because it was initially suggested to give him a court martial but he had never been into any trouble before so his CO (Commanding Officer) said to allow him treatment, long story short my dad was admitted into a rehabilitation center for substance abuse and the program was for 8 weeks, about a 2 hour drive from where we lived. My mom was required to join him the last 2 weeks of his program for treatment and therapy sessions too. She had to take off from work because she was working at the PX (Post Exchange) in customer service on a different post. I was in school and my brother in daycare, so provisions were made for adult supervision for us through the post advisory on short term care for families during emergencies and/or hardships. We interviewed a few couples, but I chose who I was comfortable with. It was a young White couple in their 20's, the husband was a soldier and the wife a stay at home spouse.

They did not have any kids. I went to school and she watched my brother during the day while her husband and I were gone. When we got to the house, she would cook dinner and I resumed the responsibilities of taking care of Damon. They were Awesome! They allowed me to drink alcoholic beverages with them as long as I promised not to tell on them because they would be removed off the list to provide their services to families. It was German Peach Schnapps nothing too hard. Miss daring and unafraid I was! Shortly after my parents returned home, my dad received orders to go to Killeen, Texas (Fort Hood) for 3 years. I realized that we really were not moving back home to Florida. We had been in Germany 1 year and we left during the summer, after I finished my Freshman year.

My mom's older sister and her husband packed our house and put our furniture in storage in Florida.

You shall not steal, nor deal falsely, nor lie to one another. And you shall not swear by My name falsely, nor shall you profane the name of your God; I am the Lord. Leviticus 19:11-12(NKJV)

Chapter Six

Living a Lifestyle of Lies

Allow me to paint the picture for you, we had all the material things that any one of us could have wanted and I did not know of any financial struggles growing up when my parents were together, if any.

We always had 2 vehicles a luxury one and a simple one. My mom drove an Audi in Germany and my dad ordered a brand new, Volvo and had it shipped to Texas. Our homes were always nicely decorated, we wore named brand clothes/shoes, and my dad made it his business to make sure we had everything we needed and wanted. I am sure that was stressful for him. This is not to brag but to depict a picture for you to understand how it was such a fraud! When we got to Texas, there was no availability on post for housing. My dad ended up getting a small 2/1 apartment in Copperas Cove, Texas which was approximately 15 minutes for him to drive to post for work. I shared a bedroom with Damon. My mom and Damon stayed home during the day. I was a Sophomore and went to Copperas Cove High School.

I absolutely hated it! I was in a culture shock again. I was surrounded by cowboys, in the country, and with racist White people. Lord have mercy! I felt like the typical teenager, hating my parents because they were screwing up my life with all the moves, and taking me through all their drama!

I was still calling back home to Florida, to talk to Antonio but he was involved in the streets by this time and around this time, I found out Pamela's twins were stillborn. Karma! We finally moved on post into housing after about 6 months, and I started going to Ellison High School, in Killeen, Texas. Finally, everyone had their own space and bedrooms, it was a 3/2.5 townhouse, with a very large front yard and backyard, on the corner in a cul-de-sac. My parents agreed that my mom would not work until she found something more rewarding for her. She was tired of working on jobs for other people, so she stayed home…walked Damon to and from school, cooked, cleaned and ran errands for us. She found great enjoyment and relaxation in planting flowers and plants, gardening and keeping our yard immaculate. She won contests for best yard due to being flawlessly manicured. My dad had completely stopped drinking and things were looking up. We no longer had company over anymore because the liquor was gone. He was going to his AA meetings and his sobriety was vital for his well-being. I had many reservations about moving to Texas, but my Junior year was much better than all the previous years combined. I was actively involved in social activities and clubs, Kiwanis Club, Speech & Debate and Home Economics where I was the Vice-President. I met a great guy that became my boyfriend, who was a Senior, worked at Killeen Mall, and had his own vehicle.

We were glued at the hip and I had him doing all kinds of things. I was sneaking to date him because my parents had agreed that I could officially date at 16 years old, but I was still 15. When they realized I had a boyfriend my dad overruled their decision and allowed me to freely date him about 5 months before my 16th birthday. My mom put me on birth control pills ASAP! I used to babysit for a young couple behind us and they were both in the military and had a little son and daughter, close in age, that I would keep so they could have date nights or just go out on the weekends. They were wild and partied with weed, cocaine, and alcohol. They allowed my boyfriend to come over to sit with me while I watched their kids and would offer us drugs to increase our sexual excitement but neither of us would partake. He was a good guy, I was daring but I was not with drugs, period! We had sex like crazy in their house when the kids went to bed.

Damon was in Kindergarten, and bad as hell by this time. He was skipping school.

How? My mom would walk him to school every morning, but eventually stopped walking him all the way to his classroom door, trying to give him some responsibility. Well, one day he took it upon himself to fake going to his classroom, hid somewhere and skipped school that day. The school called to see if he was out ill and my mom explained that she had walked him there. She had to double back to see where he was, and he was outside playing. Man, she had her hands full with him at 5 years old. He was a spoiled rotten brat and got his way with all of us in the house. My mom would beat him, but it never seemed to work out for long. She decided on being an entrepreneur and studied for the Real Estate exam but did not pass the first time and ultimately decided on becoming an independent life insurance agent with Met Life in 1986. I was still a Junior in high school, and I assisted her with Damon, household chores and cooking dinner because she was doing field trainings with her manager and learning the business.

You have allowed me to suffer much hardship, but you will restore me to life again and lift me up from the depths of the earth. You will restore me to even greater honor and comfort me once again. Psalms 71:20-21(NLT)

Chapter Seven

Pandora Box Opens

One night, I was awakened out of my sleep to yelling and crying. I got up, walked to my parent's bedroom, opened the door and my dad was straddled over my mom with an iron over her head saying that he would bash her brains out. I was yelling at him to stop! He put the iron down, then puts both of his hands around her neck and started strangling her. I told him to stop and to get off her! He was yelling at me to get out, and I started cussing him out like they had never heard before from me, MF"s and so on because I clicked! I had been cussing since 3rd grade and my mouth was vicious, but only the kids outside knew it if they tried me. He released her and I stayed in their bedroom. I asked her if she wanted to come back to my room, but she said no, that she was leaving. I waited until she got dressed and left the house in one of the cars. My dad went downstairs pissed off, to the living room and smoked a cigarette. He smoked most of my life in the house, which was so disrespectful! He and I were arguing for the first time. He asked me, who do you think you are? I said, I am that muthafucka that is not afraid of you and if you try me, you will find out! I told him that I would call the MP's on him and get his crazy ass put out of the military and he would be in worse trouble! I was tired of all his bullshit and beating on my mom! Also, I was tired of all their secrets! My sweet and innocent baby brother never woke up. I went back upstairs to my room, to go back to sleep but I could not because I was so upset! I called my boyfriend and told him what happened, which was the very first time I had confided in anyone about the Domestic Violence in my household. I felt so alone! After a couple hours, my dad left the house for PT. When it was time, I got Damon up for school, washed up, dressed, and fed him breakfast, by that time my mom was back to the house because she knew my dad was gone and she had to walk him to school. I asked her what was going on and why did all that happen? She was very vague and said he was upset but it was all in his head. Huh? What lady? I was thinking to myself you have got to be fucking kidding me! I was over it! All this time, I thought my dad was abusive to her because he was a mean drunk, but he was not drinking at all anymore, so I realized he had anger issues, but what was making him so angry was my question? I left for work and school with a heavy heart. This was the first time since the incident in Germany and it was close to 3 years that had passed. This whole ordeal was way too much for me to comprehend and I was always being put in the middle of adult situations and I did not like it. I felt like I was being punished for existing!

My Senior year rolled around, and my mom convinced me to do some things that were fun, like going to the Homecoming and Prom, in which I had never gone because I thought it was corny. Andrew was so gracious to be my escort, he had graduated the year before me. I was so miserable and unhappy, and I showed out on him at both events. I was mean and I got worse due to my family issues. However, I was privileged, to be chosen by 2 of my favorite Black female teachers, who were both members of the best sorority in the nation... Delta Sigma Theta, Incorporated, Debutante Ball in May 1987. This by far was the highlight of all my high school years combined. My parents and boyfriend were all present and the men dressed for the Black-Tie event in tuxedos, both men danced with me, but the Father/Daughter dance was priceless, and it shocked the hell out of me that my dad showed up.

He gives strength to the weary and increases the power of the weak. Even youths grow tired and weary, and young men stumble and fall; but those who hope in the Lord will renew their strength. They will soar on wings like eagles; they will run and not grow weary, they will walk and not faint. Isaiah 40:29-31 (NIV)

Chapter Eight
Falling Apart

Andrew became a correctional officer, and I was having a difficult time with him being gone. I was sick of my parent's issues, filling in taking care of Damon, cooking, cleaning, and whatever was needed. I even had to iron my dad's BDUs (Battle Dress Uniform), I felt like a slave at times! My dad was very old school and felt he only needed to work and provide for us; therefore, he did not assist with household chores, period! He would fix things that needed repairing around the house and the vehicles. My mom and I always prepared his food, took him his plate and when he finished eating, got everything without him moving. He was definitely a male chauvinist in my eyes! My dad was also racist and forbade me to date anyone White and he said no White man was welcomed in his house.

One day, I remember going into the storage closet upstairs looking for something I needed and found a journal of my mom's from when she went to rehab with my dad in Germany. I read it and discovered that she had involvements with other men. Of course, I had suspected this since I was a little kid, but she always introduced everyone to me as her friend.

What do you say or do to your mom? So, the pieces of the puzzle started coming together and my head was spinning! I was always on her side and defended her because she was a victim of Domestic Violence, which is No Bueno! However, cheating on your spouse and constantly committing adultery is a great injustice to my dad and an abomination to God! I also read that my dad had a son before me. He had gotten a girl pregnant in high school before going off to the Air Force. He had contacted the young lady, but she had gotten married while pregnant and had given her son her husband's last name and did not want anything to do with him or any support in any way. I tell you, the secrets that the older generations keep and the bones they carry are disgusting! I have a brother out there in the world somewhere that we were never given the opportunity to meet. So sad and pathetic! I confronted my mom about the things I read in her journal, she admitted to me about the older brother, but would not disclose anything to me about her infidelities. Most times, I would ask her mature questions, she would respond that I was too young to understand. I wanted to scream out loud, bitch what? You guys are screwing up my whole fucking life! I had so many thoughts rushing through my head about graduation, what colleges to apply for school, what major should I study, did I want to marry Andrew (we dated 2 years), or just move back to Florida on my own, so I could finally leave their crazy asses behind!

  Late one night, I had a terrible migraine headache, which I had suffered with off and on since elementary school. I took some Tylenol, quite a bit. This was in March and my graduation was in May. I attempted to commit suicide by taking the Tylenol, while everyone was in their bedrooms for the night. The next morning, I was not up for work/school and my mom tried to wake me up, but I was not coherent. Finally, I came around just a little to speak and she questioned me about what was wrong? I told her I took some Tylenol. Instead of her calling the ambulance, she took me to the ER because she did not want to draw any attention to our house or get my dad into any trouble. Let us talk about brainwashed! I would not have given 2 fucks about him, if my baby needed emergency care, call the damn ambulance lady! What a joke! I was taken back immediately, checked my vitals and was rushed straight to ICU. I was in bad shape! I was there for 24 hours then moved to a private room and stayed in the hospital 3 days. My mom was told that if I had not been brought in when I did, I would not have made it. But God said not so, I shall live and not die! My mom visited me in the hospital, brought me clothes, a stuffed animal and flowers with a card. My dad never came to see me. I was deeply hurt because it was all due to him/them. I remember a Black male doctor came into my room reading my chart, but once he looked up at me, he walked out of the room. Once he returned in less than 10 minutes, he asked me if I knew why he walked out? I replied, no sir, he said that he was not expecting to see a beautiful Black girl in here. He said, we don't usually do things like this. He asked, what is so terrible going on to make you do something like this? I became very transparent and brutally honest with him (first person outside of Andrew) because I needed and wanted help dealing with my parent's chaos. He suggested that I start going to therapy and asked if I had gone before? I replied, no I had not. He said that both of my parents would need to go with me, then eventually I would do my sessions alone. Well my mom was onboard, but my dad never came.

He said he was not going to no counselor and that he did not need help! What an asshole! My mom pleaded with him because I needed their support. Nothing! I started out going once a week then every other week, my mom and Andrew came to sessions with me. He was a gem! I loved him but gave him hell due to all the dysfunction I was surrounded with. I really did not know how to feel or love for that matter. I graduated from Ellison High

School, May 1987 at 17 years old. My parents, boyfriend, and my uncle (mom's baby brother) and aunt that is from Texas came to my commencement ceremony.

SN: My mom has 4 brothers…the oldest I never knew much about him, but the other 3 are mad cool! My uncle that passed 6 years after my mom was my buddy because he stayed with us in Tampa, when I was about 10 years old. My uncle that lives in Texas, his wife became my favorite aunt in high school because she and her family were warm, welcoming, and loving like my mom was and they loved us. We visited them often while living in Texas and they cooked the most food I had ever seen for Sunday dinners.

For the LORD will not cast off forever.
But though He causes grief, yet He will have compassion according to the abundance of His mercies. For He does not afflict from His heart, nor grieve the sons of men. Lamentations 3:31-33 (MEV)

Chapter Nine

Turmoil to Tragedy

Shortly after my graduation, my dad received orders to go back overseas, to the exact same place, Kitzingen, Germany (Harvey Barracks) from 1987 to 1990. Ughhh! I told my dad that I was not going back to Germany with them because I was out of school and grown. He was firm about me going back with the family. Andrew was taking about us getting married because he had a good job that would support us. I talked to my mom about it and she said no ma'am! Lastly, I thought about going back home to Florida because I applied to The University of Florida, in Gainesville. Go Gators! My dad left for Germany before us. We stayed behind until our house was packed up by the military and shipped to Germany, then we went to Florida on vacation, to visit family and friends before going back overseas. When we got back, there was availability to move into post housing right away. In January 1988, I started school at The University of Maryland and studied Fashion Merchandising. I still was not sure about what I wanted to do because I initially wanted to go to Med school until I learned how long that would take, no thank you! There were no open positions on Harvey or

Leighton Barracks, to work at the daycare centers. My first job in Texas, while in high school, I worked at a daycare care center in Harker Heights, Texas with preschool and Kindergarten ages. I ended up working at Burger King on Harvey Barracks for 9 ½ months. My mom continued with life insurance sales and was working closely with her manager, due to being overseas and learning a new demographics but same market, military families, and less civilians. My dad was gone often, to the field per usual, or on assignments. Damon was in school and I was taking classes on another post, Larson Barracks not too far from my job or home. It was another difficult time of adjustment for me because there were not many dependent kids my age. The people my age were soldiers or wives, but I was neither. There was a young married couple that lived in the middle stairwell in our building, who I would babysit for. They had a little boy that had a baby crush on me. I could not leave his sight without him crying! The husband was in the military and the wife worked on post. They were from NYC and had a homeboy over there in the military too, his name was Bam. He and I did not get along and argued all the time like sister and brother. Well one night, we all went out to NCO (Non-Commissioned Officers) club in Nurnberg, which was a 45-minute ride, and we fussed the whole way there. Tommy and Toya laughed and cracked jokes at us the whole drive. Once we got to the club, Tommy paid admission for he and his wife, Bam paid for himself, and I paid for myself. I stayed away from him and went dancing. Then he came over to ask me what I wanted to drink? He bought me a drink, and we danced all night until it was time to leave. We started dating about a month or two after that night. He had a friend at Geibelstadt Barracks with him named Ronnie. Bam and Ronnie had a great idea for us to go on a double date one night. I was the only one with a whip, so I picked them up, then to pick up Ronnie's girlfriend Fallon, who was at school. We went to a nice Greek restaurant and to the movies to see School Daze and we had a blast! She is 2 months older than me, but I graduated a year before her. I was the little big sister because I always protected her. She is tall, light-skin and gorgeous like Vanessa Williams, who talked a lot of noise, but was not fighting anyone. Fallon's mom only trusted her to hang out with me because I was a good girl. I don't not know what she saw in me, but I was the hellraiser and feisty one that would fight in a minute. Fallon and I went to the NCO club in Wurzburg on Leighton Barracks almost every weekend. She lived on that post, in Officer's housing because her stepdad was a Major. Before long, Bam showed me his true colors after a few months of dating. He was always getting into fights with other soldiers and very jealous. He was always paranoid of other men talking to me and watched me like a hawk. I am a free-spirit, and I cannot deal with someone clingy. I knew a lot of people because of my dad being a First Sergeant, mom selling life insurance, I went to school, I worked on post, and I went out every weekend. One night, while we were all together at the NCO club, a guy I knew from Larson Barracks was in the club. He spoke to me and tried to have a conversation, but I told him that I couldn't talk because my man was in there. He said, he didn't care! My boyfriend saw the whole conversation and ran over and told me to go outside, so Fallon and I went to my car. Well, they shut the club down fighting that night...Geibelstadt Barracks versus Larson Barracks. Insane! The MP's came and some of the guys were arrested that night. Ridiculous! I told her that I couldn't take it anymore and I ended our relationship after 7 months. Shortly after that, Fallon's stepdad got orders to return to the US, so we only had a little over a year to be together in Germany and I was sad again.

  My dad met a guy named Donnie at the bowling alley one day and they talked and came to realize they were cousins. Donnie was married too. My dad introduced us to them, and Donnie and Laura ended up living in the building to the right of ours. She was 5 years older than me, pretty, a sweetheart and super intelligent. She became my confidant and go-to person literally for everything and my beloved sister/friend.

  She would help me sort out the soldiers that liked me or that I dated, with all their BS! I could hear her now, she would always say to me, Dana be careful, and I love you! She had a baby girl named Tiarra that I would go over to their house to play with and sometimes babysit her. My friend Fallon was gone, and I ended up meeting sisters whose mom was in the military, they were all from Charleston, South Carolina. We were the Three Stooges, Kendra, Shandra, and me. Wendy (their mom) liked to cook, drink, and have all the guys over from the barracks, to play Spades or Dominos, eat and have fun. They had a homeboy from Charleston named Jay, who was tall, dark, and handsome. A real ladies' man and he saw me at their house one night and tried to talk to me. I kept seeing him come to their house because I was over there every day, and also at the NCO club. He kept shooting his shot for months. I told Kendra that I could tell deep down he was a good dude, but he was too much of a player for me. She told me that she was going to hook us up because it sounded like we were both interested in one another. He came over to her house one day and we had a great conversation and talked for hours and surprisingly we had quite a bit in common. He was a PK (Preacher's Kid), and they are always the worst (from my personal experience) and he hardly went to church while over in Germany. I guess from growing up in church and being made to go, it was exhilarating to be away from home. I was not saved yet but went to church almost every Sunday. He kept asking to take me on a date and one day I finally agreed to do so. It was something that I would never forget! He lived on post in the barracks, but he asked one of his Officer friends to borrow his quarters to invite me over for dinner. He made steaks, baked potatoes, and salad, with wine, beautiful flowers and a card for me. Everything was so lovely, and I was completely in awe! The time and effort poured into me was much appreciated because he worked that day too. He made the arrangements for the private time, bought the grocery and cooked.

Hello somebody! We had an engaging conversation and kissed for the first time. He still chased me for a minute, and I would not have sex with him for a while. I finally said yes to dating him and he left all his hunnies alone. We talked every day and were together as much as we could when he was not in the field. Our relationship developed organically and quickly. We had mad chemistry, and in no time, we were both in love with one another. I have always felt like he believed that he loved me more than I did him, but that certainly was not the case. I just was very reserved and sheltered my feelings. I was head over heels for him and finally I had a good one!

My parents were still having issues and arguing often and were not sleeping in the bedroom together. They went weeks and sometimes months without talking at all, and I would always follow suit with what my mom did. If she did not talk to him, I didn't either! He would come home to his chair, ate dinner there and slept there. I would occasionally hear my mom late nights on the phone having phone sex with someone and I knew it was not my dad because he would be in the living room asleep. The disrespect was at an all- time low, the audacity! She started talking to me about the idea of divorcing my dad after 21 years of marriage. I told her that I would support her decision if she was serious and that she should have left a long time ago because Damon and I were directly affected by them, especially me. I grew up in their dysfunction from the womb!

We were in Germany close to 2 years and she decided to go back to the US on vacation by herself for 2 months (November to January). She missed all the holidays with us and celebrated her 40th birthday while gone too. My dad was an emotional wreck, but my brother and I were okay.

My dad had started going to Bible Study and church with Laura's mom more frequently. He was really trying to get closer to God and build a better relationship with Him. My parents were not saved and went to church seldom. My mom could care less about going to church. I was the one in the house that went to church faithfully, although I was not saved either. I continued business as usual, cooked, cleaned, took care of my brother, went to school and work, spent time with Jay and my friends. My dad watched Damon if he was home while I went out. He blew me away when Thanksgiving rolled around because he cooked a feast, collard greens, mac and cheese, dressing, rice, yams, potato salad, baked ham, and fried chicken, all from scratch. I asked him where did he get the food from? He said, he had cooked it. I said, all these years we have been slaving over cooking for you and you know how to cook? Man please! He started a conversation with me, crying and pouring his heart out. He told me about how he had taken care of my mom her whole life and he loved her more than anyone even himself. I told him that was his first mistake because you cannot love someone more than yourself. How can you give from an empty place? Imagine a

19-year old young lady almost 20 the next month telling a 44-year old man about life. God has given me spiritual insight and wisdom from a kid.

On Saturday, February 9, 1990, I had to work from 8:00am to 5:00pm, to do an infant and adult CPR class for work. My regular schedule was Monday through Friday 6:30am to 3:00pm and I worked primarily with preschoolers, but my job included adults in the training. When I got home and walked in the door, it was very eerie! I saw a stack of papers on the coffee table when I passed to go to my bedroom. After a few minutes of being in the house, my mom asked me to go for a ride with her. While we were talking, she said that Meeks had received the divorce papers in the mail, but he hadn't said much to her. When we left and were driving down the street, my dad came out of nowhere and tried to run into our car with his car, right in the neighborhood. What the hell! I knew he had lost it because he never involved me in his foolishness! Those demonic spirits had taken occupancy because he could not take captive of his own thoughts for months with Biblical principles and I saw what was taking place. The enemy wanted to destroy whomever he could use. We were able to dodge the hit and Meeks backed up and went back home. All that and Damon was outside playing and never saw any of it. My mom said to me in the car that she was getting a place and we would be moving in 10 days, she was buying herself a Jaguar, and paying for me to go to college. I asked her why did she come back? I told her that Damon and I were fine the whole time while she was gone to the US. She said everyone was telling her the same at home because she had visited Florida, NYC, and Texas, and for some unknown reason she did not take the sound advice and came back to Germany. However, she did say to me that she felt like Meeks might try to harm her, but she had put in place a large insurance policy on herself. My dad and I were the beneficiaries.

  I went to my room to relax and was listening to Maze and Frankie Beverly and started taking down my posters off the wall. I had fallen asleep across my bed. I was awakened by my mom yelling out, Dana Help Me! At first, I wasn't sure because I was in a daze, then I jumped up and ran into my parent's bedroom. This was February 10, 1990 at approximately 2:30am and when I opened the door, my dad was straddled over her while she was lying on her back, stabbing her with a kitchen butcher knife. My dad weighed, easily 230 pounds, my mom 135 pounds and me at 115 pounds. I was silently praying in my head asking God what do I do Lord? I went up to him and put my right forearm around his neck and pulled, nothing happened. So, I did it again, and his whole body with his feet in the air came off the bed! God's supernatural strength was released in me! My dad's face was swollen, eyes bloodshot red, and sweating profusely. He had on a white T-shirt and yellow cut off sweatpants. My mom had on her night gown and scarf on her head. I was the only one still dressed from the day before because I had dozed off. My mom rolled off the bed onto the floor and got up and ran to the front door and collapsed, with the door wide open. By this time, I was cussing my dad out to the top of my lungs! He was yelling for me to call the ambulance as he was trying to find clothes to put on. My brother woke up immediately from the disturbance and stayed at her side on the floor in his pajamas. Many of our neighbors came out of their houses, but our neighbor directly across from us put blankets on her to keep her warm because she was a bloody mess. She told me, Meeks tried to kill me and passed out! I LOST IT! I started screaming at him telling him to get the fuck out or I would kill him! He stepped over her and passed everyone and left the house. I was FURIOUS!

I ran next door and told Laura, and came back and called my friends (Kendra, Shandra and Wendy) who lived in walking distance and I called 112, which was the emergency number like 911 is here in the

US. The Polizei and the ambulance arrived instantly because there was a German hospital across the street from us. All this happened in less than 15 minutes from the time I woke up. The paramedics were taking my mom out of the house when Kendra, Shandra and Wendy got there. The Polizei dispatched the MP's because we were on American soil, in which they had no jurisdiction.

No weapon that is formed against you will succeed; And every tongue that rises against you in judgement you will condemn. This [peace, righteousness, security, and triumph over opposition] is the heritage of the servants of the Lord, And this is their vindication from Me, says the Lord. Isaiah 54:17 (AMP)

Chapter Ten

Devastated

The police got there and were asking me nonstop questions and I was answering as if God was downloading my brain like a computer chip. God has given me a gift to recall information, especially numbers like times and dates on demand. I remember license plates, Social Security numbers, and birthdates well. I also have a photographic memory. Damon was quiet the entire time from the time he woke up. My neighbors took him across the hall to their house to attend to him for me. The Crime Scene Unit came and taped off our house with crime scene tape and it was so surreal. I felt like I was in a movie. They asked, where did I think my dad would go? I said I did not know, but I thought that he may try to commit suicide. I gave them a description of the vehicle and license plate number. They asked, what caused this whole ordeal? I explained that my mom had filed for divorce and my dad had just received the papers, which one of the officers saw them still lying on the coffee table. The papers had been there all day from when he got them out of the mailbox. It seemed like I was being questioned for hours and I was devastated and exhausted! They would not allow me to remove anything from the house, to take clothes or anything until the investigation was completed. They asked, if I wanted to stay in a hotel? My friend Kendra said, no officer, she can stay with us before I could reply. They also asked if there was someone that could come from the US to be there with us? I said yes, I would call my mom's oldest sister. This aunt could afford to come at short notice. She and her husband along with my parents were the couples that would financially assist others in the family when needed.

I called and spoke to my aunt briefly and explained what had transpired and apologized for calling with such bad news. She replied, I am coming! Once Damon and I got to Kendra, Shandra and Wendy's place. I told their' mom Wendy that I needed Jay with me ASAP! She replied, I'm on it! Since she was a soldier she knew what to do, and contacted his Battalion and The American Red Cross got a word to him because he was at the Czech border going on an assignment and they got a message to him that he needed to return back to post. Jay had no idea what happened. Why was he allowed to come back and were not married? Maybe because my dad was a First Sergeant on the same post with him, and everyone knew of my dad. Listen to me, the favor of God is real because God knew I needed my village of people that loved me with me during that time. Once he returned and came to me at Wendy's house, I laid my head on his chest and screamed out a piercing cry! I cried and cried some more, and he just hugged me tighter and tighter. He stayed with me every day. He went to work on post and came back to me. He was my love and my heart, and I needed him. I still did not talk about what happened in my house that night (early morning), not a word to him for about 3 days. I just took care of business and my brother. I took him to school every day, trying to keep some normalcy in our lives, but I don't think it really helped at all. At that time, Damon was 9 years old, soon to be 10 and we experienced hell on earth! The incident was on AFN News (Armed Forces Network) for days and I was mortified! I would never in countless lifetimes would have imagined that my family would be on the news for such a heinous crime and depicted in such a way like this. On the outside looking in, we looked like The Huxtables, but on the inside, we were each going through our own form of hell! I really tried to stay neutral the majority of the time because I wanted to understand both of my parent's points of view, and I loved them both dearly. I just could not understand why stay in a domestic violent relationship and adultery. What sense did that make? Damon and I were victims and suffered silently, although he was shielded from a lot because God protected him by keeping him asleep or outside playing while most events took place.

My dad had turned himself into the police at the Wurzburg station, after a few hours of leaving the house. After being detained there for many hours, he was transported back to Kitzingen to Harvey Barracks which was his post. The police called me to come to the station to identify him. When I got there, I identified him from looking at him from another area. They asked me if I wanted to speak to him? I replied yes, and he was brought out to me. I told him that my aunt was on the way and Lorene is in the hospital. He asked me was she okay? I replied, I trust God that she will live!

SN: Something interesting to know, I never called my parents mom and dad, but Lorene (first name) and Meeks (our last name).

My aunt arrived in 2 days because she had to go to Miami to get an emergency passport first then fly to Germany, which is approximately a 10-hour flight and the time difference to Germany is 6 hours ahead of Eastern Time zone. This aunt was my childhood role model because is intelligent, an educator, pretty, well-dressed, and always has nice things. Mrs. Bougie! She decided to stay alone in a hotel, to process and pray. My mom had lost an extreme amount of blood and there was no more blood in the local blood bank, therefore blood had to be flown in. By the time my aunt arrived, my mom had surgery to somewhat stabilize her injuries and was flown from the German hospital in Kitzingen to the German hospital in Wurzburg, to the trauma unit, due to the severity of her stab wounds. After another surgery, she was transported on post to the American hospital where she stayed and had to undergo her 3rd surgery because most of her internal organs were punctured by the butcher knife…heart, lungs, small and large intestines, one kidney, spleen, liver and pancreas, therefore she was in bad shape! My aunt was with me every move I made and was praying with me, that was her baby sister would survive. I can only imagine how she felt. I called Laura's mom and another mother from her church and they joined us at the hospital to pray as well. My faith was on a 1000% because I trusted God with everything! My mom was in the hospital a total of 3 days and all 4 of us were there every day (me, my aunt, Laura's mom, and the mother from the church) praying for her healing and recovery. She was put in a private room after surgery. All of us went in to see her, but she could not have a conversation due to being connected to all the machines. One day while we were in her room praying, I was by her face and she squeezed my fingers softly and my aunt was at the end of her bed by her feet and saw her move her toes. God was confirming to us that she was aware that we were there with her and she was not alone.

Well on February 13, 1990, my mom passed on the 3rd day in the hospital and we had not gotten to the hospital yet on that day. I was running errands, taking care of business, and picking up Damon from school. When we got back to Wendy's house there were 3 people waiting there for us. I asked, why are these people here? I had Damon go in one of the bedrooms and I went in the living room where they were sitting and they explained to me that my mom had passed and asked me if needed them to tell my brother? I replied no! I would tell him myself. I called him in the living room and told him Lorene had passed. He asked, what does that mean? I explained to him that she died, and he burst into tears! I had to stay strong and comfort him, so I did not cry. On God, that was so very difficult for me. The case workers left, my aunt stayed awhile, then took a Taxi back to her hotel. When Jay got off work and came to the house, I finally cried in his arms in Kendra's bedroom privately because I did not want Damon or anyone to see me breakdown. The next morning, we went to the hospital so I could identify my mom's body, but she had already been moved down to the morgue. We all (my prayer warriors) went down to the morgue, but my aunt and I were the only ones to view her body and say our last goodbyes. This was the first time I had been in the morgue or seen a dead person. No words can express the emotional state I was in. I was shaken to my soul, the very fiber of my being!

More Devastation!

Do not rejoice over me, my enemy;
When I fall, I will arise;
When I sit in darkness,
The Lord will be a light to me.
Micah 7:8 (NKJV)

Chapter Eleven

What Are You Saying God?

The AFN News had gone from attempted murder by a military soldier, to murder and the world seemed to know everything that happened to my beloved family and the rumors spread like wildfire!
HUMILIATION!

I was in the Shoppette (convenient store) on Larson post one day, in line behind 2 ladies talking about the whole ordeal not knowing I was the daughter. They were saying that my dad had caught my mom in the act of cheating on her husband. I said very loudly, that is not true because I am the daughter and I was there, were you?

Total embarrassment on their faces! Point…keep your fucking mouth closed if you don't have facts! My mom was making 6- figures, smart, beautiful, a First Sergeant's wife, drove a 745i BMW (German specs, so faster than American made) and an independent life insurance agent who was widely respected in the community.

I was driving around town running errands like crazy. My head was spinning and overwhelmed because I had to prepare for a Memorial Service and the pre-trial before we could leave the country. I had to withdraw Damon from school, plan for our house to be packed up and shipped to the US, decide what to do with 3 vehicles, go into our house to get her clothes and find photos for the service, continue to answer questions for the authorities, go to the bank to get money and close out accounts, and try to manage my own business and I had to keep everyone updated. My dad needed clothes for the pre-trial but this time I could not stomach going back into the house and had someone go in for me while I waited outside. During the 2 weeks that I was still in Germany, I had to finalize a series of events. Everyone was quiet and focused and very supportive to us. My aunt was my shadow because I needed her to keep my strength. Damon did not ever say much and was at Wendy's house with Kendra and Shandra, who watched him for me in my absence. They cooked, made sure he had a bath, and I was always back before bedtime to assure that he slept with me every night. I was his only comfort during this horrible situation. I was so blessed and grateful for everyone involved, they were all heaven sent by God to help us. My dear Jay was my rock and was there with me through it all along with my friends. Love is very interesting and a rare experience. My mom's Memorial Service was beautiful! It was held at the chapel on Harvey Barracks and was filled to capacity, standing room only and people (military and civilian) were outside to the street to honor her and give their condolences. My beloved Jay, brother, aunt, Kendra, Shandra, Wendy, my cousin Laura, her mom, the mother and my mom's manager and his wife were all seated up front with me. I had chosen only 1 photo to be presented in the chapel for the service. Many people spoke on her behalf of where they met, or when she sold them life insurance. They spoke on how knowledgeable she was on the products, which enlightened them on the importance of having life insurance. They shared very fond memories of her, and my heart was full. I felt so blessed and grateful that her life was so impactful in such a positive way. After the service, I had to deal with the pre-trial, which was only 3 days after the Memorial Service. I had seen not seen my dad since the night of the incident. We (my prayer warriors) saw him being escorted into one of the rooms near the waiting area with handcuffs and shackles on, by the police officers, prior to going in the courtroom. I asked if I could speak to him? They allowed me, my aunt and the mothers who accompanied me, to pray with my dad for Salvation and he accepted Jesus Christ as his Lord and Savior. I asked the guards if I could touch him, they said yes. I gave my dad a hug and told him that I loved him. No emotion or response, which was usual but at that time, I am certain he did not know how to feel or how I felt about him, due to the circumstances. Once we entered the courtroom, the pre-trial began and it was very detailed, and graphic to say the least! I had to relive every moment of that night and identify all the bloody photographs because I was the only witness. My brother did not have to take the stand because I informed the judge and court that he did not witness any of the violent act. He literally stayed on the floor by our mom's side, until she left by ambulance. After I testified, the court suggested giving my dad the death penalty or natural life in prison. I testified that he was temporarily insane because he was indeed. The devil had taken over his mind before he received the divorce papers, but the day he received them... he snapped! It is so vital to take captive of your thoughts and feed it with the Word of God. My mom had included that she wanted part of his pension, child support, alimony, and full custody of my brother.

Greed! Greed! Greed!

Commit your works to the Lord, and your thoughts will be established. Proverbs 16:3 (NKJV)

Pride goes before destruction, And a haughty spirit before a fall. Proverbs 16:18 (NKJV)

The curse of the Lord is on the house of the wicked, But He blesses the home of the just. Proverbs 3:33 (NKJV)

We had a grueling 3 days in court, Damon and I were summoned to return back to Germany in 6 to 8 weeks for the trial to sentence our dad. I prepared to go to the US, when we got back to Wendy's house, I asked if someone would go back to my house with me, to clean up before I went back in to pack our suitcases because I could not stand to see the blood and mess everywhere. It was very emotional and painful to go back inside, but I had to do what I had to do. While in there, I inventoried all of our belongings because I had a weird feeling. The military was coming in to pack our household and ship to the US. After I settled that evening with my love Jay, I called all my friends that played an important part in our lives and said my goodbyes.

Heart-wrenching!

Many are the afflictions of the righteous: but the Lprd delivereth him out of them all. Psalms 34:19 (KJV)

Chapter Twelve

Trying to Make Sense of It All

My aunt, brother and I left for the airport. Damon and I had on sweatsuit and jogging suit and sneakers, he had a jacket, and I took my mom's full-length blue fox coat and fur hat because I didn't want it stolen. We flew to Orlando, Florida and waited for our luggage, but no luggage showed up! We were told maybe it was on another flight and they would contact us once our luggage was retrieved. No call, so I called a few days later and our luggage was never found! We moved in with my aunt and her family. She, her husband, and their youngest daughter, who was a Senior in high school. They had 3 children, their older daughter lived in Miami and their son, the oldest lived in Atlanta. The girls grew up sharing a bedroom with twin beds, so Damon and I occupied that room and my cousin moved into the guest room. This was a big adjustment for everyone because it was such a sudden change without much notice. Hence when you have a close and loving family, they would make the necessary adjustments with love and not with resentment. Now Damon and I were in a new place and had to get acclimated without our parents for the first time. He was in the 3rd grade and just a baby. I had just turned 20 years old and had an enormous responsibility which was gut punching! The pain I felt was too much for me to articulate into words. We were at the mercy of others because we were starting over from scratch and pretty much with strangers because we never stayed with anyone. My parents raised me to work hard and have my own things and if I had to use anything of others, I had to replace theirs and get my own too. Therefore, us not having any clothes, shoes and underwear was humiliating! We tried to fit into a new family dynamics and environment, which was very challenging to say the least. Damon and I could not sleep due to having nightly nightmares for months, due to the trauma we had experienced. We suffered from PTSD. I continued to be to the same consistent person for him with everyone trying to help us get adjusted, but honestly Damon and I both felt like we did not fit in anywhere. This side of the family was not loving and warm. I had always felt this way as a child, even before my brother came along. Everything felt cold and forced with them. The money I had did not last long from my last couple of payrolls. Everything in my mom's name was tied up until the insurance company completed their investigations. My mom's Social Security benefits went to Damon because he was a minor. I looked for jobs immediately, due to not having anything, I had to wear my cousin's clothes and I shopped at Garage sales, Goodwill and Walmart.

I was at my lowest and it got worse not better! I had to study to get a Florida Driver license because I never had an Operator's license in Florida. I had to take the written test and driving test. I did not pass the first time on the road with parallel parking. I also had to wait on my car to be shipped from Germany, so I was at the mercy of using my cousin's car. We all had jobs and had to get back and forth. So much confusion and drama!

I had to plan my mom's funeral soon after getting back to the US. Met Life released funds for the services. I solicited help from both my aunts and delegated tasks because I couldn't do everything. This was the first funeral I had ever planned or attended and it was the toughest thing I had to do! My grandmother, brother, and uncle (mom's oldest brother) did not attend the funeral and stayed at the house. Damon was scared and I told him that he did not have to go, no one could ever change that she was his mom. They all were still in shock! My grandmother mourned my mom and my dad because she raised them both. The funeral was at my grandmother's small Pentecostal church down the dirt road from her house, and again it was standing room only. The church was filled and overflowing out to the street. Jorge came but never came inside the church. I never saw him, but I was told that a gentleman was outside crying and from the description I knew it was him. I kept the funeral closed casket at the church and at the grave site because she had been expired almost 3 weeks. The repass was at my grandmother's house and it was like a family reunion. I was completely numb and cannot remember who was all there and honestly did not care because no one had experienced what Damon and I did.

  The 3 of us went back to Germany 2 months later, April 1990, for our dad's murder trial. The trial was not as difficult for me as the pre-trial because I did not have to relive all those graphic photos again. Damon and I both took the stand and were asked character questions. The things we enjoyed doing individually and collectively as a family. When Damon had to testify, they went easy on my baby and were considerate. Thank You Jesus! My dad looked the same, blank stare with no emotion. Due to his excellent service record, he was not given the death penalty or natural life in prison because I had proven temporary insanity.

  I remember when I was 8 years old, I went to a revival with this same aunt in Plant City, Florida. I recall seeing a lady standing at the altar, with a swollen face and sweating profusely, while the Pastor was praying for her. The lady was demon possessed and several demons were occupying her body and started speaking through her, each demon had a different sound/voice. I was in astonishment, although not afraid. The Pastor tarried with her an hour or longer. Once he rebuked all those demonic spirits out of her, she ran around the church in celebration and every time she passed us her face went down more and more from the swelling. I remembered that when I saw my day stabbing my mom to death that night. Meeks was sentenced 60 years in prison with the possibility of parole at 25 years. My heart skipped a beat, throat got dry and my stomach was instantly sick. We lost both of our parents in a moment! We could not have ever prepared for this in a million years. The blessing in it was he did not kill all of us and himself too, which is what we constantly see nowadays in the news and on social media.

Food for thought: In all bad situations, it could be worse!

Back in Lakeland, I found a few different jobs until I liked one enough to stay more than 30 to 60 days. One weekend, my cousin and I drove to Miami to visit her sister that was in school there. It was my first time going to Miami and I loved it! I only stayed at my aunt and uncle's house for 6 months (February to August) then moved to Miami with their older daughter who I had just visited. I automatically had it in my plans to take my brother, but they agreed to let him stay with them, therefore I could concentrate on school and try to regain being normal again, if that was possible. I was apprehensive but appreciative at the same time. My cousin and I got a 1/1 apartment together with a 12-month lease, her mom cosigned for us with both our names on the lease due to us being young and no strong credit history. We bought new and used things from many places to furnish our new place. We were given the twin beds from their old room that Damon and I used. My car was shipped from Germany, so we shared my car, went to the same school, and worked in the mall at Burdine's (now Macy's) just different departments, too much togetherness and it was a real trip! After 10 months of that, I moved out and got my own place but in the same apartment building. We lived on the 3rd floor and I moved up to the 9th floor. I continued to pay my half of the rent the last 2 months to be fair because my name was on the lease too. I had gotten the insurance proceeds from my mom's death. The proceeds were split 50/50 with me and Damon. My dad had to be removed as a beneficiary because he caused the death. Damon's portion was put into a trust account, due to being a minor, until age 18. The period before getting the money was challenging and all I heard from family members was about the money. I confided in a few friends of ours in Germany about the situation. It was a sad time for me and so much confusion and drama. When someone dies, many families, are usually divided and always looking for something for free and my family was no different. I was young, naïve, a people pleaser, and wanted to show my appreciation, for the support given to us. I paid cash for a brand new 1991 Mazda 626 LX in the fall of 1990. I am practical and simple. People were throwing out names of all different luxury cars, and I was like nope! I gave my uncle, their son and both daughters money. The cousin I had stayed with money to buy a used car. I gave another cousin from my mom's middle sister my old car that was shipped from Germany. This aunt I gave our furniture from our house in Germany and whatever she wanted. I did not want any reminders from that horror! Once our things were shipped to Mac Dill Air Force Base, in Tampa, I had the opportunity to go through our things, and most of our valuables were missing or stolen (i.e. China, Crystal, Porcelain dolls and masks) which was another upset. I had an estate sale after allowing family members to take what they wanted first. I only wanted my mom's China and Crystal that I repacked myself and labeled the boxes in my writing and stored in my aunt/uncle's attic for 25 years. When I finally did get my things, my aunt had unpacked a couple boxes and taken out and used what she wanted without getting my permission and I noticed it right away.

  The saga continued and kept getting worse! I gave my grandmother money and paid tithes to her church. I believe in giving and paying tithes and offerings. I am a giver naturally but for some reason I felt obligated to do for them. One uncle went to jail and no one had bail money, so they called me to borrow it and I never saw a cent of that money back, which was at least a couple stacks. My aunt that I stayed with would not take any money, but I always bought her nice gifts for holidays and special occasions that she did accept. I was always running up and down the Turnpike from Miami, to Lakeland, and Tampa to see my brother, family, and friends. I felt like the freaking ATM, but no one was turning down any financial help from me. I did not give any cash amounts under $1k and I kept the receipts to remember because people will play amnesia like they cannot recall your acts of kindness.

  Once I was settled in my own place, my beloved Jay was back in the US, he came to visit me frequently in Miami, on the weekends and sometimes take additional days, to make the visit longer. We always had an absolute blast together! Every time he came, we did fun things like shopping, fine dining, clubs, movies, beaches, sightseeing, and whatever we felt like doing. I loved spending time with him because our time together was easy and enjoyable. He was my security blanket from Germany. I loved spoiling him and surprising him with nice gifts. He proposed to me in Miami, but could not afford the engagement ring, so we looked at rings together and decided on a 1.5 carat solitaire that I purchased, and he promised to pay me back when he could. It worked for me, no biggie because I am not materialistic. We were excited and he wanted me to meet his family in Charleston, South Carolina where he is from, so I flew there one weekend and got a hotel and rental car. He picked me up and I went to meet his parents and siblings at their home. They were very nice people, and we had a good time together. However, there was a situation over the weekend between his mother and I that upset me. I asked Jay if we could talk privately? We went outside in the yard and I explained what transpired in the living room and I asked to leave. He drove me back to the hotel, and he stayed with me and I cussed all the way there. I will say this, while in Germany his mom always wanted him to buy her gifts (hats, shoes, and perfumes) and I had an issue with it because he could not afford to do those things she wanted, but I honestly did not think he could say no to her. He and I both are the firstborns and I have much respect for his role in his family. I too did the same things for my family. However, I have studied about marriage growing up because it perplexed me due to witnessing such terrible marriages around me. A couple weeks after being back home in Miami, we spoke on the phone in great detail about the situation again and I told him that once we were married I would come first and I realized that he would not be able to choose me. I broke up with him on that call. We dated from 1989 to 1991, over 2 years gone just like that and I was so heartbroken! I was already broken from my parent's issues and needed him to choose me. Did not happen!

More rejection!

First, and last time that I have been to the state of South Carolina. My only fiancé to date and I literally checked out after that with men and started dating a few men at the same time for years. I only cared about my brother…Period!

  I met Nadine at Burdines, we worked together in the Jr. department together. It was her part-time jig because she worked full-time at a bank during the day. I asked her about getting me on and she invited me to an Open House. I got hired on the spot for a Teller position and quit retail. I worked in Surfside (located on Miami Beach) and was the only Black in the bank. Nadine was from St. Croix and loved Reggae. I started going out with her to Ladies' Nights for Reggae Wednesdays at Strawberry's. I went out full-time, school full-time and worked full-time. Thursdays was Miami Nights, Fridays was Luke's on Miami Beach and Saturdays was back at Miami Nights and Sunday was Big Daddy's 119. I was a ticking time bomb, but no one knew it! I took care of business at school, made good grades, always punctual at work, and church, but partied, and shopped a lot as a coping mechanism, always a trendsetter but was miserable trying to camouflage the hurt and pain. The men wanted me, and the females were influenced by me or became my haters, either way I did not give AF! I worked out daily and drinking heavily. I was living the life in Miami! However, 2 years later, one night I tried to commit suicide for the 2nd time, by taking pills, drank liquor and Clorox bleach. COMPLETELY NUTS! One of my close friends kept calling me on this particular night, but I did not answer her calls. She discerned that something was terribly wrong, and she and her friend Bob drove to my place and climbed 9 flights of stairs to my apartment and banged the door down! Finally, I became coherent enough to get up and let them in, and she realized what I had done because there was a big mess in there and vomit on the floor. She called 911 for the ambulance and I was taken to Jackson Memorial Hospital. Chellie and Bob came behind. My stomach was pumped, but I had already thrown up most of the toxins, before getting to the hospital. I was at Jackson for many hours for observation for before suggesting that I be admitted but I refused to stay. Chellie told the doctor I could stay at her place and she made sure I was comfortable and safe. I met Chellie through her brother because he and I dated for about 7 months, in 1992. It was a love-hate relationship, but very passionate. Me being nice and a great girlfriend, I co-signed a pickup truck for him and we were both in college. Well I broke up with him due to his lies and cheating, so I paid the loan off because I could not trust that he would make the payments and I did not want my good credit in jeopardy. He never paid me anything and got a free vehicle. *More rejection!*

Blessed is the man
Who walks not in the counsel of the ungodly,
Nor stands in the path of sinners,
Nor sits in the seat of the scornful;
But his delight is in the law of the Lord,
And in His law he meditates day and night.
He shall be like a tree
Planted by the rivers of water,
That brings forth its fruit in its season,
Whose leaf also shall not wither;
And whatever he does shall prosper.
Psalms 1:1-3 (NKJV)

Chapter Thirteen

Transition

While in Miami, Damon faced many challenges (bad temper, fighting, lying, and skipping school), therefore I had to move back home to Tampa, December 1992. Miami was not the place for a troubled teen to live. It was my first time back in Tampa since we left in June 1983.

SN: I had been in communication with Antonio and he would come to Miami to visit on his runs and I would come to Tampa to hang out with him. I was in my new apartment less than 30 days and someone broke into my place through the bedroom window and went out the front door. I was only gone for 4 hours, to run errands and get a new Driver's License. My furniture sofa and loveseat, TV, Stereo, as well as all my friends and family photos, and 2 sets of diamond earrings that were cleaning in alcohol, which were previously my mom's, were all stolen. The police said it was someone that knew me or had been watching me.

I have always believed it was a guy that worked for Antonio because he was my next-door neighbor, and he would see Antonio coming over to my place often.

More heartbreak and loss!

I had transferred my job with the bank and got a large moving company to move me from Miami to Tampa into my apartment. Damon had stayed with our aunt/uncle in Lakeland, aunt in Dade City, cousin in Tampa and a group home, but no one could help, therefore it was my reason for moving back. We tried counseling for him, but he was not cooperative. He shared with me that he told the counselor whatever they needed to hear to get through his sessions. Once he was out of the school, the summer 1993 we went to visit our dad for the first time. He had been at Fort Leavenworth, Kansas, (Military Penitentiary) for 3 ½ years by the time and Damon I went to go visit him. I had forgiven him within the first 2 years because God always forgives us for constantly screwing up. Who was I not to forgive?

And whenever you stand praying, if you have anything against anyone, forgive him, that your Father in heaven may also forgive you your trespasses. But if you do not forgive, neither will your Father in heaven forgive your trespasses. Mark 11:25-26 (NKJV)

I remember asking him what happened that night? Meeks never explained why things happened the way they did, but he took full responsibility for his actions. Overall, our trip was decent, the hotel, rental car, and the little sight-seeing we did. The visiting days were long at the prison. Damon said he would never go again to see him. I had a conversation about it later in the hotel room, but he was not hearing me. On the flight back home, Damon said that if Meeks ever got released from prison that he would kill him! Umm…what? Sad truth, my dad said he knew Damon felt like that and if he came at him, he would have done what he had too! I never said a word and shook my head at the realization of the enemy's plots on my family.

  He started the 6th grade when school started and straight out the gate he was getting into fights. I was getting calls from the school all the time and having to leave work. My discernment said to me, our visit to see our dad was not good for him and added more fuel to the already burning fire. Boys process differently than girls, also he was much younger and a little boy when everything went down. Damon was being a protector of our mom and taking her side and I understood his point, however I was not taking sides and supported my mom on her views, and I supported my dad the best I could. Damon stayed with me less than 6 months because he was out of control and too much for me to handle. My aunt researched a great military academy in

Melbourne, Florida that was super expensive, but I got the funds approved from his Trust. He was not there a complete term and got expelled for fighting. He got expelled from 4 different counties in Florida...Polk, Pasco, Hillsborough, and Brevard. The struggle was real! It was very painful going through all of this with him because I felt his pain too. He was already a spoiled brat, but I wanted to ease the pain, but nothing helped. When he lived with our aunt/uncle I paid for him a nice bedroom set and Wave Runner. My aunt sold them when he moved out without asking for my permission or just checking to see what I wanted to do with the items first because she did not purchase any of them. Damon had whatever clothes and shoes he asked for, but his attitude and behavior were reckless. Money cannot buy happiness! Long story short, he ended up going to Gainesville, Florida to live with one of my uncles (dad's younger brother) and his family, after years of trying to work with him. Before long, he was not going to school and coming in late nights and they were not with it either. My baby was growing up fast! He eventually dropped out of school in the 10th grade.

SN: I was in Tampa less than a year, one day Antonio and I were together all day, from breakfast to dinner. He had spent the night before with me. I had a prophetic dream about him, that the Feds were coming to arrest him. The next morning, I kept calling and paging him, but no response! I went to his auto body shop to tell him about my dream, but he was too busy to talk, due to the phones ringing and customers coming in and he told me to tell him about the dream when I came back from Lakeland. I went to Lakeland and on my way back my pager was blowing up with codes and 911. It was mid-morning and when I got back to Tampa, the Feds had already arrested him and I boo-hoo cried!

I never had an opportunity to tell him about my dream until I went to visit him a few days later. I had known him since I was 5 years old, friends since 10 and dated him at 13 and loved him so much.

More heartbreak!

God covers us in our disobedience, however there are still consequences to walk out for being disobedient...let that sink in!

If they obey and serve Him, They shall spend their days in prosperity,
And their years in pleasures. But if they do obey,
They shall perish by the sword,
And they shall die without knowledge.
Job 36:11-12 (NKJV)

Chapter Fourteen

Blessing and Curse

Shannon was one of my friends from 11 years old, her uncle, who was a minister and loved the Word of God. When I would go over to her grandmother's house, he and I would talk about life and God. He discipled me in the Word and helped me understand God's principles, then I started going to their church, Cathedral of Faith. I got saved and baptized in February 1994. It was 4 years after my mom passed to the month. I finally felt some level of peace and was very excited about giving my life over to Christ. I went to church every Sunday and every Wednesday for Bible Study. I loved hearing and studying the Word of God. In April, I moved back to Miami because my brother was gone and I certainly did not want to stay in boring Tampa, because I loved Miami. I shipped my things again, transferred back with my same bank and was out! My friend Chellie was attending a Mega church, New Birth and I was obsessed with going there, it was the who's who in the church world back then. My spirit was getting fed and I met awesome people. I stopped going out, stopped drinking, and no sex for almost a year. I was happy to finally make some progress.

The next year in February 1995, I was in a friend's wedding that lived in Miami, who was from Lake Wakes, Florida. I went to Tampa, which was an hour away. The word on the streets was one of the guys I grew up with on my same street had good dick. I linked up with him that weekend and I got pregnant for the first and last time. See how the devil always tempts you with your weaknesses. I was crushed because we used a condom that broke but I thought I was good. My friend girl Ana who was a medical assistant at a doctor's office did a pregnancy test for me at her place, it was positive...I fainted! I called Fallon later that evening upset, and she stayed on the phone with me all night until daybreak to convince me not to have an abortion. The next morning, I had a well-women exam already scheduled and I did not say a word. The nurse came back in the room and asked, Ms. Meeks did you know that you were pregnant? I said, yes ma'am. She was so excited and hugged me and that made me excited! I was scared to face people and especially at church, but I did not stop my normal routine and continued going to church. The hate that I received from the older Saints was unbelievable! I was in utter shock, by their behavior and how I was received due to being saved, single and pregnant. We all fall to sin at times, but we must keep our eyes on Jesus, repent, and pray to break that thing that hinders us. My addiction was sex! Everyone's issues are different. I held my head high and read my Bible and Psalms 37 daily to give me strength, and I looked pass them like they were invisible. I had a friend that was a minister at the church and I never would forget her telling me, they are talking about you but will never discuss their skeletons, like the abortions and other women's husbands they have slept with, so keep coming to church girl.

Although I was very sad and depressed while pregnant, God blessed me to have a beautiful pregnancy, no morning sickness, no food cravings, no swelling (nose, hands, feet), flawless complexion and normal weight gain of 30 pounds (125 to 155).

By this time, my mom had passed 5 years and I was accustomed to abandonment, rejection and going through tough times alone. The love that was given from her remained a thing of the past. However, I have friends that have adopted me into their families wherever I have lived. Damon was 15 years old and still having difficulties and came to visit me in Miami, while I was pregnant. We had a great conversation about what we experienced individually, and our views were so opposite. He looked at life as a joke because of the challenges we faced. I had the need to conquer the adversities and not become a victim of them. Nevertheless, I told him he needed to get his act together because he was headed for destruction if he did not change his way of thinking. I completely stopped communicating with my baby brother because I needed a break and a peace of mind. Tough Love!

On November 18, 1995, I was given the greatest gift that I could have ever imagined, Taylor Tiarra Wynn was born and changed my life forever! I was 25 years old and turned 26 the next month. I had close friends who are identical twin sisters, one was my supervisor at the bank and the other became my Lamaze coach and go-to person about motherhood. My due date was November 21st, but I knew in my spirit that I would go into labor when I did because my body felt different. I got up that day and cleaned my house, did laundry, and went to the Broward County Fair. I was always known to do everything alone (eating out, movies, shopping, outdoor festivals, museums etc.) and I walked around and bought things to eat and after about 45 minutes I felt strange. Oh boy, I had to get out of that fair and quickly! I got home and was putting up my laundry and my water broke. I called my Lamaze coach and she advised me to call my doctor and I said nope! Maybe about 20 minutes later, she called me back and I still had not called, so I called my doctor and was advised to go to the hospital. She picked me up and we laughed all the way to the hospital because I was cracking jokes per usual. Once at the hospital, I was still playing around and taking the pain from my contractions like a "G" because I have a very high tolerance for pain, but baby when that pain starting hitting my back, tears flowed down my face. My Lamaze coach ran and called the nurse into the room and said she is in too much pain! The nurse said we are waiting on her doctor to get here, because I cannot deliver her. I said, if no one delivers my baby now I am jumping out of this window! She went to scrub in, and on her return my doctor was with her and said Ms. Meeks you are ready to have this baby quickly for your first one. No response from me because I wanted to strangle him! The entire time from my water breaking to delivering Taylor, was less than 8 hours. Many mothers are in labor for 12-24 hours with their firstborns. Lord, thank you for being with me!

My aunt from Lakeland came to Miami and stayed with me almost a week to help me and out and I was very grateful. I was in a new role without any parents, grandparents, or any siblings living in Miami with me. I forbade the baby daddy to come, no need for a homicide to take place! Jesus was and is a way-maker! I gave in and allowed him to come see his daughter at 2 months old. I was breastfeeding and ate Jamaican food with cabbage not realizing that it would give me and my baby gas. Taylor kept crying from the discomfort, so I called my Lamaze coach. She asked me to backtrack what I ate for the day. I told her and she said Taylor had gas and to get Gripe water for her. I sent baby daddy to Walgreen's in my car because he came on a one-way bus ticket to Miami, in which I had no idea at the time. He left in the car and came back in less than 10 minutes. This nigga tells me that he does not have any money, also can I buy him a beer too? I gave him a $20 bill and said bring my change back. Once he got back, I asked him how the hell can he come see his child for the first time without any money? He told me this lame ass story about he was waiting on some money to come. I said nigga that is the oldest story in the books. In a conversation he confessed to me, he put a hole in the condom that night and he always wanted to marry me and have kids. I said you have got to be fucking kidding me! I have never liked you or dated you! I said do you have a bus ticket back home? Because you have to get the fuck out my house! He replied no, I said I will buy you a ticket and you need to leave, first thing in the morning. Morning came and I dropped him off real early at the bus station, sit there and wait. Bye MF!

SN: He is diagnosed bipolar and was in and out of the mental hospital before I had any dealings with him. But I was not sure if the rumors were true. Well, at 7 months pregnant he called me from an institution in Tampa and told me that he had no clothes and money. I asked about his parents and siblings, he said no one would come. I figured that they were all burnt out from all his shenanigans over the years, I was so kind to drive from Miami to Tampa about 3-4 hours to see him. I bought him clothes from Burdines (now Macy's) and put money on his account and sat awhile and talked with him. When I was walking out, a doctor asked me, ma'am are you okay? Would you like to sit down and have some water? I realized everything I needed to know about him that day, which was be done Dana!

Damon called me after 2 years of us not speaking and asked if he could come stay with me and I felt something different in my Spirit said yes immediately. I had been moving around Miami for 7 years (1990 to 1997) and finally God said enough, and I purchased a nice 2/2 condo in Miramar, Florida and remodeled it without help from anyone.

SN: God revealed to me that I psychologically moved so much because I had to move often as a military kid.

I was a supervisor at the bank at the this and was doing well, however the struggle was real being as a single mom.

Damon was 17 years old and my daughter Taylor was 2 years old and his very first time seeing her. He was immediately head over heels in love with her and she was crazy about her Uncle Damon! He came to Miami, the Spring of 1998 and he turned 18 years old in July and finally got his money from his Trust. He literally balled out of control! He did not listen to anything I said to him. He told me that he was doing whatever he wanted with his money and he was not helping family and friends like I did. He talked me into getting registered guns for us in my name, he paid for two 9mm. I also took the concealed weapons class but never got my photo taken for it. In November, he went to Florida A&M University's Homecoming, in Tallahassee, Florida and got drunk, pulled over, DUI and jailed, with one of the guns in the car. Of course, I bailed him out of jail, and got his car out of the impound. The police told me I had to physically come to get my gun from Tallahassee. I said okay but no thank you! When he returned to Miami, he had to get his own place because I had a toddler, in school and his lifestyle was much too disruptive for me. Late nights and smoking weed everyday was not my cup of tea. We found him a house to rent about 2 miles from me, so I could get to him quickly if needed. I was always on edge with him and high alert! In the same month, November he and his girlfriend went to the Florida Classics, which used to be in Tampa but had moved to Orlando. She is from Deland, Florida and went to Florida Memorial College in Miami. A few days after the big game, tragedy hit again. My babysitter told me when I picked up my daughter, she said your brother came by here today. I asked her what did he do or say? She responded, he just sat here awhile and played with Taylor. I said oh okay, he didn't call or text me when I was in class. It raised an eyebrow but okay. I went home, cooked dinner, fed and bathed Taylor, and watched television a bit. It had gotten late for me between 10:30pm to 11:00pm and Damon called me, seemingly upset and said…I am leaving! I asked where are you going now Damon? I will go with you! He said, I love you and Taylor. You guys are the only people I love, then I got it! I started pleading with him that there is nothing to hard for us to overcome together. God has delivered me twice from this, not saying the word suicide. He said, I am not you and I can't forgive Meeks! He said, I have never done drugs before and I did tonight. I asked where he was, and I would come to him.

He said, I am in a motel in Gainesville and hung up on me. My phone rang less than 5 minutes later, and his girlfriend said, Damon just called me saying he was leaving, then I heard a loud noise like a firecracker! I started screaming...he is gone, he is gone! Then she started crying. I told her that I had to call my aunt in Gainesville (dad's brother's wife). I called her and explained what happened and to call 911 and to go find my brother and call me back immediately once she knew something. I was in shock and the deepest pain you can imagine, but I was still hopeful that he would be okay. I got off the phone with my aunt and called his girl back. I asked her if she wanted to leave with me? If so, I would book the flights ASAP! She said yes and the flights were booked from Fort Lauderdale to Tampa. I called my aunt in Lakeland and told her what I knew at that time. I scooped up Q the next morning from campus and dropped off Taylor at my cousin's for the weekend until I returned because I didn't know what I was going into. Once at the airport, we were waiting to board the plane, my aunt in Gainesville called me and said they found Damon. I asked, is he okay? She replied, he is dead...he shot himself in the head! I LOST IT! I slid to the floor sobbing! Then Q started crying but still trying to help me. Everyone was coming over asking how they could assist me? I simply said, please do not let the flight leave without me! A flight attendant came over after several minutes and said ma'am we have held the plane as long as we possibly can. We finally boarded, I was still crying, and I sat by a Black guy, who was a comedian on BET. He said I cannot imagine what has you so upset because you lost it out there, but God will take care of the situation for you. I looked up at him listening because the Holy Spirit was present and speaking through him. He said, if you trust God, you will make it through this. I started calming down and we talked until I dozed off to sleep because I hadn't gotten any sleep the night before. We got to Tampa safely jumped in a rental car at the airport then drove to Lakeland. Once at my aunt's house, she, her 2 daughters, Q and I headed to Gainesville. My aunt in Gainesville kept me updated on the police activity and the investigation. I was adamant about going to see the motel room where the incident happened, but the Coroner's office had already taken him, by the time we arrived. I became HYSTERIAL! I wanted to see the room for myself, but everyone was telling me that it was better not to because I had experienced enough trauma! We waited around for several hours in Gainesville and I was contacted about funeral arrangements and I gave the family's funeral home in Dade City, who buried my grandfather, mom, uncle, grandmother and then brother. Once we got back to Lakeland, Q and I jumped back in the rental car and went to Tampa to visit before heading out. I made a phone call to my childhood friend Shannon's mom's house, and I told everyone what happened, so they were there waiting when we arrived. I needed to contact my dad at the prison, to inform him but did not have the nerve to do so. Shannon called for me. The warden said, I will have the chaplain call you right back with the inmate and to be by the phone. The chaplain had my dad with him, and I had to explain to him what happened…my dad cried! This was the 2nd time in my life he cried to me. I LOST IT! Shannon had to take the phone and talk to the chaplain for me. The chaplain offered his condolences and said that if I needed to update my dad on anything to call and ask for him. When I got back to Miami, I fell into a deep depression. I never went back to work and I was a supervisor at a bank. My job sent me a Fed Ex letter to ask if I was returning and I signed it No! I could not take care of myself or my daughter. After a few days of not responding to anyone, my friend Chellie came to my place and packed us up and drove us to her house. We stayed with her about 2 ½ weeks because I could not get out of the bed for anything other than to use the bathroom. I was not eating, showering, nothing and cried all the time! I did not want anyone to see me like that. Chellie totally took care of my daughter for me. You name it, she did it! Man, when I tell you, God has blessed me with awesome friends, who are my family, and I am forever grateful (past and present). One day, Chellie decided that I needed some answers and help, so she took me to a Cuban man in Hialeah that practiced Santeria. I told her that I was not dealing with no witchcraft! She assured me that he did not use his gift for bad and evil, nevertheless I went to see him. We went into his house, and he prepared his altar then took me in the living room and cleansed over my whole body with something burning (maybe sage). Afterwards, we sat down on each side of the table and he took my hands and stared at my face. I did not ever say a word! He shared with me what had transpired with my mom, dad and brother. He said that my brother was very sad before he died, and he wished that he could have my strength. He said that Damon would not accept the call of God, but I would. He also told me that I had been depressed for a long time, but the devil would not win. I would always overcome his tactics. He told me that I would move again but out of the state of Florida, going North. I cried the whole time because I knew his gift was real. We should always try the spirit by the spirit.

Beloved, do not believe every spirit, but test the spirits, whether they are of God; because many false prophets have gone out into the world. 1 John 4:1 (NKJV)

Shortly after visiting him, I got my life together and planned my brother's funeral, which I decided to do graveside only. I could not bear another Memorial Service or church funeral. My mom and dad's people came to his funeral and my friends from Tampa. I had the service closed casket as I did for my mom, but people kept asking me to see him. I could not understand why people will not respect your wishes. Black people get on my nerves, but I love them! I told the funeral director to allow viewing once I was away from the casket, but he opened it before I was completely out of the way. I saw my brother in my peripheral view and fainted! My uncle that was there with his wife from Texas caught me before I hit the ground. There were several of us riding in the truck together to the repass and my uncle from Texas said, God gave you Taylor to save your life because you would not have made it after Damon died. The Holy Spirit was saying the exact same thing to me at the exact same time, he just spoke it audibly. I was in tears again...can you say heartbroken!

Those things, which ye have both learned, and received, and heard, and seen in me, do: and the God of peace shall be with you.

Philippians 4:9 (KJV)

Chapter Fifteen

It Got Worse

When I got back to Miami, I had to go clean out the house Damon stayed in and noticed that some of his jewelry, AK-47, and his 2 pit bull puppies were gone...MIA! I knew exactly who to go to. The house was owned by a Haitian man that stayed in the main house and my brother rented the side house that had a bedroom, bathroom, living room, a kitchen and den area. No one had house keys but him and me. I went to him and asked did he have my brother's belongings? He tried to lie but I told him I was calling the police on him. He returned the jewelry but said he did not have the gun or the puppies. He had gotten rid of the puppies...liar! Well I had a guy friend go in the house to get clothes and Fed Ex them to me for Damon's funeral who admitted to taking the gun and offered to buy it from me when he realized I was not giving him the gun in my name. So, I eventually sold it to him because I could not use it. Man, I went through it dealing with people. I had to keep my scruples and sanity because my anger issues ran deep, however my faith and hope in God sustained me. I never considered committing suicide again. Hallelujah! Did the enemy try me? Yes, on every side and every angel because I dealt with deep anger issues. I put the devil under my feet and trampled on his head with the Word and prayer! I had to keep my spiritual crew around me, pastors and prophets that were my friends. God has always allowed me to keep company with clergy men and women everywhere I have lived. I kept busy with work, school, church, and motherhood. The pain became insurmountable! My anger issues got worse and I had to get therapy to effectively address it head on. One of my friends from church, A Place Called Hope, was a counselor by profession so I went to her and she helped change my life. She gave me tools to use, to help me process when I felt myself getting angry. One year later, my daughter and I were leaving a Christmas program at church, that she participated in, on our way to Blockbuster then home. I was on the phone talking to my boyfriend Darren. Taylor was asleep in her car seat, but I told her to get out and lie down on the seat because she had a crook in her neck. Moments later, a Dulley, pickup truck hit us from behind on 441-North and caused a 5-car accident going forward, due to the impact on my car. 3 cars ahead of me were involved. I couldn't find my phone and my daughter was screaming, but I couldn't see her, my head was woozy, and I kept shaking it not to blackout, but I could not find my baby! Someone called Miami-Dade police and they were there in a flash! I remember a Hispanic female cop, who came to my vehicle to check on me and I told her my baby was in the car, but I couldn't find her. She tried opening my door but could not get it opened. She went back to the driver of the Dulley, who was also Hispanic but male and cussed him out! She came back to my vehicle and I was able to find Taylor and pulled her very slowly from the fold of the backseat. Long story short, me following the Holy Spirit and instructing her to lie down saved her life because my car was totaled, the bumper and trunk was pushed in to the front seats of my car. The cop pulled Taylor out of the driver's side window and the Jaws of Life had to cut me out! We went to the hospital by ambulance. Darren had come to the scene because the called dropped with no answer afterwards.

  He knew my location because I told him I was on my way, to drop off the movies before heading home. Once at Parkway Hospital, we were separated because they took my daughter to Pediatrics and me to ER. She was screaming because she could not see me and, I said absolutely not! So, I declined to be checked out by a healthcare professional and went with my baby. Shortly after my accident, my job went out of business. I was working for El Palacio Hotel in the banquet center, as an Event Coordinator, only the banquet center closed.

The Holy Spirit told me, to move back home to Tampa. I was like nope because I love Miami! I got a brand new 2000 Nissan Xterra and only had it for 6 months then repossessed. I had my Mazda almost 10 years and paid for, therefore I was not accustomed to having a car payment, but that was not the case I just did not have income coming in. I have always been very responsible and believed in paying bills early and definitely on time. My accident, loss of employment and repossession, then due to not having income my mortgage got behind and I was only making partial payments, to try to recover.

The Holy Spirit kept telling to move, but I did not want to move and stayed in disobedience. My friends threw me a rent party at the hotel to raise funds, but still not enough money. My realtor found a buyer with good credit who also had the resources and was approved. God pulled the plug and shut the whole deal down…condo foreclosed! It was unexplainable to everyone, but I knew what was going on. If I sold my condo, I would have had the money to stay in Miami, but God said no! The plot thickened…Darren and I had been friends since the early 90's, but he was also a ladies' man and I would not have anything to do with him for years. When my daughter was 6 months old, we started dating in 1996 until we moved to Tampa in 2000 (it was off and on) due to his cheating. He had been staying with me for about 3 months, by the time he became MIA quite frequently and not answering my calls and pages. We were pass the honeymoon stage of going out to comedy shows, concerts, work functions, get-togethers with his friends, and wining and dining. I had a friend named Nia she tried to duplicate everything I did (hairstyles, clothes/shoes, car, condo etc.) but she was my dawg for years from 1991 to 2000. I would go to her house and I would always see her pregnant neighbor and would speak to the lady and have small chit chat convo with her. Well unbeknownst to me, Darren and Nia were keeping a secret from me, her pregnant neighbor was pregnant from my man and neither of them had the courage to tell me. The betrayal and hurt I felt…Instant Rage!

The night Darren finally told me, I jumped on him and told him that I would kill him! He never touched me and went into the bathroom to get a wet paper towels to try to stop the bleeding and left. I called her and gave her the business and told her I would beat her ass the next time I saw her! This transpired on a Wednesday night and that Saturday morning, I was moving out of my place without anymore said.

Shannon, her then fiancé (now husband), her cousin and her husband all came to move me back to Tampa. They paid for the

U-Haul and their aunt paid for the 1st month rent of my storage unit. Darren had been calling me, but I did not answer because I was moving. He came over when we were literally putting the last items on the truck, looking at me in disbelief. One thing about me, I don't play with words, if I say something...I mean it!

SN: The take-away from this...when God speaks, listen, and obey! Slow obedience is still disobedience!

And He said to me, "My grace is sufficient for you, for My strength is made perfect in weakness." Therefore most gladly I will rather boast in my infirmities, that the power of Christ may rest upon me. 2 Corinthians 12:9-10 (NKJV)

*Though I walk in the midst of trouble,
You will revive me;
You will stretch out Your hand
Against the wrath of my enemies,
And Your right hand will save me. Psalms 138:7*

Chapter Sixteen

Putting the Pieces Together

I moved back to Tampa, September 30, 2000, this time with a child, a sad day it was for me...Jesus! I thank God I had a calm and easy-going child. She was always a good kid for me. I just could not ever seem to get it together after my mom died, an emotional roller coaster and I wanted to get off! We stayed with Shannon and her daughter Jade in their 2/2 condo. We occupied Jade's room. My homeboy Derrick who I mentioned in a previous chapter, allowed me the use of one of his vehicles, to have transportation to look for employment etc. He owned a restaurant and made sure we had a meal when needed. A friend of his, who became one of his baby mamas and I became friends through him. They were my angels sent from God! In October 2000, I had been asking around about good churches in the area. I went to a Mega church, Bible-Based of Temple Terrace and really enjoyed the service that day and I joined the first visit.

  The Pastor walked straight down the aisle to me during his invitation and the Holy Spirit prompted me that he was coming to me. I met some phenomenal women there. They helped me with life, babysitting Taylor because she attended the church daycare and elementary school. They would pick her up if I needed, until I got off work. I had a difficult time re-adjusting.

In November 2000, I started working at Mercantile Bank and not too long after working, I bought a cash car, a used Honda Accord from a childhood friend's father-in-law. It was a lemon, no AC because it went out after 2 weeks and always breaking down, but it got me around town for 2 ½ years. One evening I had gone to the hairdresser after work and had left food in my car from lunch. When I returned there were roaches literally everywhere!

There were freaking roaches in the floorboards! I had to bomb my car and not have food in there EVER again! Who knew roaches can get in the car? Geesh!

My branch manager took me under her wings. She was an older White lady and very strict, but I was okay with strict because I liked order. I always reference ethnicity/race to explain and show diversity and inclusion because I truly love everyone. God has always opened doors for me as a young Black lady. My parents taught me well. I adopted my mom's out-going personality and my dad's discipline and structure. I met Diane, a pretty, well-dressed, real cool, and jazzy lady at church, and one of the Trustees, who had twins and they would watch Taylor for me sometimes as well. Diane and I were kindred spirits instantly and she's one of the sisters of many that God has blessed me with because I never had any biologically. January 2001, she started her own Women's Ministry named Sisters in The Spirit Ministry, Inc. I was fortunate to gain many sisters over the 10-year span. They all have been God-sent. It was a spiritual game changer for me, and I am Forever Grateful!

SN: Pay attention to times and seasons with people because all are not required to go the distance with you, many are temporary, and a few are lifetime. God will bring people in and move others out, so don't get caught up in your feelings like I did.

In February 2001, I was able to move into a 2/2 apartment, but due to having a foreclosure on my credit the deposit was pricey and I did not have it. First time since my mom died in February 1990, (11 years to the month) I asked my aunt in Lakeland for her help, but she said no! However, her husband loaned me the money to move. God will always make a way! Shortly after moving in, my dad called to tell me about his niece that attended The University of South Florida and we went to meet her on campus, very nice young lady. Once school was out for the summer, she needed a place to stay in Tampa because she was working.

She stayed a while and slept in Taylor's bedroom, if I remember correctly, she did not stay the entire time that she needed too. I treated her poorly as if she was in my space, just the same as Damon and I felt at my aunt's house. It was a vicious cycle, and it was pathetic on my part and it was not okay! I felt terrible and talked to my dad about it in person at a visitation. He had been transferred from Atlanta, Georgia to Wildwood, Florida in 2002.

When I spoke to her again, I apologized for my behavior and asked for her forgiveness. She and I are close to this day. Since I did not grow up being around them, it took a few years of growing pains for us all to mesh and understand one another but let me tell you, they are the warmest, most loving and genuine people. Just simple down-to-earth country folk from Newberry, Florida, and I love me some them!

After I had my daughter in Miami, my doctor told me that I would need to have surgery in the future, due to fibroid tumors. In July, my doctor in Tampa suggested that I have a hysterectomy at 31 years old. I literally broke down crying at the doctor's office and my branch manager had to come get me. When I got back to the bank and finally calmed down enough to talk. The other ladies suggested that I get a 2nd opinion. I did get the 2nd opinion and I ended up having a myomectomy instead.

On August 2001, on Taylor's 1st day of Kindergarten, I had my surgery and had no medical issues, no prior surgeries and no medications. I was thinking what if something happens to me, who is going to take care of my baby? I had major trust issues with most people, but I prayed because I had to trust someone to take care of Taylor for me, while I was in the hospital for 3 days. One of the teachers at the daycare filled in for me and she had kids too. My branch manager cooked and prepared meals for me once I got back home. Many church members and friends came over as well. It takes a village, and I was blessed!

In February 2002, when income tax time rolled around, I got a Cashier's check to repay my uncle for the $2k I borrowed from him to move. I called him and he said, it was a gift because you and your baby needed a place to stay. I was in tears and graciously thanked him from the bottom of my heart. Father God, I thank you!

I went out with Shannon one night to Club Moet. I did not want to go but she begged me to go with her. Welp, I met an amazing man that night, named Stewart. He said he saw us come in the door and followed me around the club until I stopped. He came over and asked me to dance, and we danced for the rest of the night. He bought Shannon and I drinks the whole night. When it was time to go, he asked for my phone number and we exchanged them. He was in the military reserves activated at Mac Dill Air Force Base. He gave me his business card on civilian job in Houston, Texas. I went to church the next day and was home cooking dinner afterwards, when he called me. We talked for hours and after that day, he called me every day to check on me and my daughter and straight out the gate he started financially doing things for us within days of meeting me. We started dating it seems like immediately, he was 8 years older than me and a perfect gentleman. Baby, we were a pair together! We dated for 2 years (2001-2003) we went to his hometown of Mississippi 2 years in a row to visit his family. He was one of 5 children and his whole family even the in-laws loved us. I finally thought I would get married.

Stewart and I had been talking about marriage, but he flipped it on me and said just move to Houston. I said nope! I was not moving to a new state with a small child on a promise. I would leave my home state, my friends, and my family...no thank you!

We ended up on the phone for like 3 hours trying to break up, but we could not say the words, so we ended up just saying goodbye. I cried all night! I was sick for months and lost so much weight.

In March 2003, on a Sunday afternoon, one of my coworkers called me to see what I was doing? I had been depressed about my raggedy car and had been walking to work for weeks and getting rides for my daughter to get to and from school. I was in fear about getting a car with payments again and she said I am coming to pick you up and take you to get you a car today! I got a 1998 Saturn with low payments and low insurance cost. Stewart and my dad helped me out with the money. Yep, from prison my dad got funds to me. Won't He Do It!

  Things smoothed out a bit for a minute, by the end of the year I had changed banks because I was recruited by my old assistant manager from Mercantile Bank, who moved down the street to AmSouth Bank as a branch manager. My mentor was so hurt but I left after 3 years because she never gave me what I was worth in my yearly raises. Tuh! I am a single mom and needed that dough, so I gave my 2-week notice and bounced. July 2005, I was at my desk at work and received a phone call, from a church member. She said God spoke to her about watching my daughter because I wanted to go back to school. I started crying because it was true, and I hadn't mentioned it to anyone yet. I enrolled in school for the Fall semester. After a few weeks in, one day she would not answer my calls when I needed to drop Taylor off to her, then she called back and said she was at the center, when we got there, no answer at the door or phone. I had to take my daughter to class with me. I had a presentation that night with sensitive content, but my professor told me that I could not stay in class. I was so hurt! She was disobedient to God and had to answer to Him!

In life, we all have ups and downs, trials and tribulations, however; have integrity people! If you say something and cannot do it, let the person know immediately. No harm, no foul! I am not a sensitive person, so my feelings don't get hurt easily, but if you lie, cheat, steal...I am pisssed off and done with you! But God, He always comes through and makes a way when people let you down!

There was talk at work about changing the banking hours to include Saturdays, each employee would rotate working on Saturday. I had enrolled in a class that I needed, but it was only offered on Saturdays. I had spoken to my assistant manager and branch manager about going back to school and my class schedule, in which they both approved was okay. I was in that class about 3 weeks and got fired because the regional manager did not approve it.

More heartbreak!

I had to move out of my apartment after 4 years and 8 months, because I had already had a foreclosure and a repo on my credit and did not want or need an eviction too. I spoke with the leasing office and explained my situation and the manager understood and allowed me to break my lease by paying 2 months of rent to terminate. The balance went to collections before I could pay it because of timing, but once employed again, it was paid it off in full! Hallelujah!

In October 2005, we moved in with Raina a widow with 2 grown children that lived alone in her 3/2 home, who went to the same church and was in the Sister's ministry with me. I continued school, going to church and dedicated to Sisters. My friends were making fun of me for being so committed to going to Sisters and my Spiritual journey. Raina and I became close…we prayed, praised, danced, and worshipped God together in that house, even laughed and cried many times sharing stories about life. Taylor was on her track team which is her ministry because she is a former college track star and Olympian. Well she had a cousin that moved from another state to Tampa, who talked her into making us move out. We stayed with her for 10 months. I had initially asked to stay there up to 12 months when I moved in because I worked a couple of different jobs before landing a better one. I was so hurt and upset, and Diane was doing everything to keep me encouraged and prayed for me. She couldn't help me because she was living at her brother's house. Diane is an amazing WOG! My so-called friends were talking shit about me bad, and some of the ones picking at me for getting closer to God included the same ones that moved me from Miami. I was displaced again!

More heartbreak!

In August 2006, we moved in an Extended Stay America paid for by our church, Jesus People Ministries. I was on the Finance Ministry and paid my tithes/offerings faithfully, so my Pastors allowed me that privilege. I was greatly appreciative and humbled! It always seemed like this very private person was always being put on display for public humiliation, but God has kept me! When I wanted to act out, cuss, and fight…God kept me focused, sane, and quiet!

My Pastors were going on a trip to China and I did not want them to continue occurring the cost for the hotel and decided to leave after 3 ½ weeks. I made a call to my aunt in Lakeland for the 2nd time. I called to ask for help. I asked if we could stay with them 1 to 2 months? She responded that she would need to talk to my uncle when he got home. I said okay. She called me back in less than 15 minutes and said that she did not need to talk to him…no!

September 2006, we ended up staying with another Sister for about 5 to 6 weeks in her 2/2 townhouse.

In October 2006, I got out of retail banking after 14 years, just not enough money and I was too smart and talented not to be making the income that would afford me a better life. I started at AFS (Academic Financial Services) a student loan company. I was there until September 2007, almost a year when our payroll checks started bouncing. It happened to me not once but twice, in which the company made good on them. The CEO was embezzling money! When my check bounced the 2nd time, I started looking for other jobs on the clock. I applied at Humana and had a phone interview at my desk while at work. The same week, I was invited to an Open House for an in-person interview. I interviewed with 2 Black females and to date that has been the hardest interview I have ever had. Thankfully, I have a 90% on the spot hiring success rate and I was offered the job. I went back to work and gave my 2-week notice.

On November 11, 2006, we finally moved into our own place, which was 1 week before Taylor's 11th birthday. We moved into my humble beginnings, Ponce De Leon income-based housing. It had been torn down and rebuilt to a beautiful imagery. Somebody say, it was still the projects, but I was happy and blessed to be there!

SN: I met a guy at AFS that was 8 years younger than me, we started dating and I let him move in and he started going to church with me. I eventually co-signed a car for him. I should have learned my lesson form the ex in college right! Well my friends from church saw him out one night at a party with another female and came back and told me. Of course, when I asked him about it, he denied it. Nigga, I believe my peeps over you because they are my fam! He got involved into some extra-curricular activities and got arrested one day while I was working. I packed his shit up and put it outside in my storage room for him to pick up, and I took the car back and drooped it off with the keys inside…voluntary repo! Deuces MF!

I have been more than generous to anyone in my life (male, female, family, family, or foe), if I got it, you got it! I have paid $700 tabs, vehicles, trips, bills, and loaned money for whatever the need was when asked, but 98% has never been recovered. We all know how it feels to need something, but God wants us to need Him first!

I have shown you in every way, by laboring like this, that you must support the weak. And remember the words of the Lord Jesus, that He said, God says it is more blessed to give than to receive. Acts 20:35 (NKJV)

God will continually bless me and make a way for me because I give and not selfish.

On October 1, 2007, I started at Humana and became a licensed agent selling Medicare. We were in training for 3 to 4 months studying to pass the licensed health/life insurance exam. It took me 4 tries before I passed (66, 68, 69, 74) with at least a 70%. The Pressure and Struggle! When God blesses you with anything, you still have work to do, it (that thing) will not just land in your lap without effort and hard work. I kept pushing forward and my eyes stayed on God!

I can do all things through Christ which strengthens me. Philippians 4:13 (NKJV)

Constantly rejoicing in hope [because of our confidence in Christ], steadfast and patient in distress, devoted to prayer [continually seeking wisdom, guidance, and strength], contributing to the needs of God's people, pursuing [the practice of] hospitality. Romans 12:12-13 (AMP)

I have told you these things, so that in me you may have peace. In this world you will have trouble. But take heart! I have overcome the world. John 16:33 (NIV)

Chapter Seventeen
Self-Discovery Mode

I remember shortly after my mom died in 1991-92, I had gone to pick-up my brother from my other aunt's house in Dade City. I overheard her saying to her brother that Lorene was cheating on Meeks and that's why he killed her, in the tune of she deserved it. Of course, I had been hearing the speculation about the reason for a while. However, I became upset because it was still a very painful situation and I argued with her about being disrespectful. My uncle stepped in and told her to be quiet. She was known to be flip with her mouth.

In 2007, my uncle (mom's youngest brother) and aunt from Texas were in town and stopped by my place to visit. My uncle told me that my mom was cheating with a man in Texas. We lived in Texas for 3 years and I had no idea of any involvement with anyone. My mom usually introduced me to her guy friends, not the case this time and it raised an eyebrow. I thought about my dad with the iron over her head that night. This news was bothersome and positioned me to start asking questions instead of overlooking everything.

In April 2008 at 38 years old, I finally had to have a hysterectomy and I was overwhelmed with emotion...confused, embarrassed, and hurt. I always wanted to get married and have another child, and prolonged the surgery for 7 years, but was no longer interested in having any more children. I had suffered female issues since my 20's, but having my female reproductive system removed was drastic to me. I went through it psychologically. It seemed as if I would never have any good outcomes in my life. One hurt, struggle, and tragedy after another, but I still trusted God! I was at a crossroad of pushing forward in ignorance or empowering myself by discovering and learning about what generational curses were hindering my progression in life from both sides (maternal and paternal) of my families. What were the causes and effects of my behaviors? What was God saying? What tools were given to me in my upbringing? What were my influences, socially, culturally, and economically, my biases/stereotypes, and my spirituality? These were all the topics I delved into after my surgery and over the upcoming years.

During this time, Diane had become a licensed Minister and was walking in her calling as a Prophet. She was my accountability and prayer partner. While I served in her ministry for 10 years, I was in her core leadership, her amour-bearer and helped bridge lasting relationships with people I knew in Miami. Taylor also accepted Salvation, at 8 years old in her Sister's Ministry.

Praise Break…Whoot Whoot!

Train up a child in the way he should go, And when he is old, he will not depart from it. Proverbs 22:6 (NKJV)

I remember my mom being so excited to turn 40 years old and 2 months later she died, which has left a lasting impression on me, however I wanted to be better than she at 40. I was so guarded and emotionless for many years. Anger and rage consumed me, but I did not want this behavior to become the new trajectory for the remainder of my life. I did not like the person I saw in the mirror and it was my mission to change that view.

In April 2010, I moved out of the hood because the kids were too bad, my daughter was having to fight weekly, and the maintenance men were coming into my house stealing my personal belongings. Taylor was at the end of her 8th grade school year and needed some normalcy again because this certainly was not it. I was having to leave work frequently due to situations happening in the neighborhood. We moved to Temple Terrace, which was my old stomping grounds as a kid. We moved to a complex that we stayed in until she finished high school.

By this time my dad had been in prison for 20 years. He was at Fort Leavenworth, Kansas from 1990 to 1998 (Military pen 8 ½ years), Atlanta, Georgia from 1998 to 2002 (Federal pen 3 ½ years) and Wildwood, Florida from 2002 to 2014 (Federal pen 12 years) at Coleman. He moved from maximum security to medium then to low all on the same compound.

SN: Antonio was incarcerated with my dad in max security for several years. Also, Diane's brother and my dad's nephew are guards at the same facility. Small world!

Taylor met her granddaddy at 2 ½ years old and I took her each time I went to visit him because they both needed that bond and relationship with one another. I took care of my dad for 20 of the 24 years that he was incarcerated. When I had stacks, he had stacks. I would send him money that would be on his account for a year or more when I could afford to do so. I visited every facility he was housed in. Whatever he asked me to do regarding his business or personal affairs was done. Anyone that has visited a Federal Penitentiary knows the process is long and cumbersome. The staff was usually rude, or just doing too much. Therefore, I had my share of going above and beyond to be supportive. It is so sad to say, our conversations were always surface and if I had a pressing matter to share, he really did not say much. I was told by my therapist, he probably felt guilty and because I reminded him of my mom and was in the house that night, he kept reliving it in his mind. I had a dad present in the house, but he was absent therefore, I grew up with daddy issues. However, I had to learn to put myself in my parent's shoes to derive to a conclusion of what ideals they may have had about family and raising children.

My dad would not tell me he loved me and that cut me deep because I am very affectionate, compassionate, and loving. I think in my entire life he told me he loved me maybe 3 times. I tell my daughter I love her all the time and throughout the day.

I greet and leave my friends and family with a hug and a kiss. I learned a valuable lesson that night of the incident, not go to bed mad. Although my mom and brother died tragically, I was relieved that they both knew how much I loved them because I said it to them whenever we spoke. I have heard many times of people regretting not doing or saying something before someone dies and they carry guilt many times for years or even a lifetime because of it. I am an advocate of counseling/therapy because it has given me the tools I needed at different times in my life. I have tried my best to apply anything that will result in a positive outcome going forward.

In 2010, I spoke to Taylor and my therapist about my dad coming to live with us when he was released from prison and they both said the same thing, it was not my responsibility and it would not be fair to me because he caused this mess. Also, because I have PTSD, as a result of the trauma and violence. I cannot deal with extreme violence in videos, movies etc. I had a conversation with him about it in person one day and that was the last day that I went to the prison to visit him. He ceased all communication with me. More disappointment, pain, and rejection!

Minister Diane had gotten married and I was one of the people that helped bring their special day into fruition...a beautiful wedding it was! She and I attended 3 different churches together outside of her Sister's Ministry. One night in Bible Study, our Pastor told us to form small prayer groups. Minister Diane, her then fiancé, another male Minister and I prayed together. God used me prophetically, while praying for her fiancé and God said through me that he would be a Pastor.

About 4 years later in February 2011, I was one of 7 people to start the church from their living room, every Sunday morning tired and all doing New Membership classes and establishing the church.

In 2010, I was approached by an IT guy at work, he asked me if I liked to dance, and I replied yes. He asked if I was interested in coming to a Chicago-style stepping classes? I was and I did, on Saturdays in Brandon, Florida and had so much fun! We had stepper sets weekly and one day in class I met a lady from Lakeland named Roni. We became cool and spent a lot of time together. One night we were at a hole in the wall in Dundee, Florida at a stepper set and I saw this tall, dark, and handsome masterpiece of a man. I said to Roni, he is fine! She said I know him and will introduce you, and I said I don't need you too, I will introduce myself!

John was 15 years older than me, never married, had one child (daughter) and was the youngest of 4 siblings. He was a correctional officer (Lieutenant) and very well-known in Polk county. I had not been in a relationship since Stewart in 2003, 7 years had passed. John and I dated almost a year and I never had to pay for anything. He was a perfect gentleman, provider, affectionate and I was his trophy girlfriend. We went everywhere together parties, step class, church, and family functions. I met his whole family…siblings, in-laws, daughter, and grandkids but he was playing games the whole time.

In May 2011, I had gone out of town with my daughter for her Spring Break to Miami and I text and called him but there was a long delay. Roni and her sister were going to the club that night, so I text her to see if John was in there because my spirit was uneasy! She responded back to me that they saw him there with another woman. He finally called me back on his way home from the American Legion and we talked for 2 hours. Well, 2 hours later a woman called my phone and asked me why I was calling John that time of night, which was about 4:30am when she called. First and last time a woman ever called me. I said bitch you ask him and don't call my phone again and hung up! I called him on his cellphone and his house phone a few times before he answered, and I went off! Of course, he denied knowing anything! About a week later I broke up with him the weekend of Father's Day, after returning the gifts I had purchased for him but still gave him cologne and a card. He continued to lie to my face which infuriated me, and I replied...I would kill you nigga! I am so sick of games and lying, therefore it was time to go Dana!

More rejection!

In May 2012, I became a licensed Minister under Dominion Life Faith and Worship Church. Co-pastor Diane and her husband's church, who is the Pastor, with another young lady, and we had a Pastor from

Orlando, Florida to become ordained. I did everything from cleaning the church, opening and locking up the church when needed, saturating the environment in prayer, praying and laying hands at the altar, covering my Pastors in prayer while praying for others, planning events, over Finance Ministry, Teens Ministry, Trustees, Pastor Appreciation Committee, and taught New Members class and was next in charge if the Pastors were out. The hell I caught from walking in excellence and being gifted!

  I know how to plan and execute, when my Pastors had an idea and I brought it to life. Shortly after being licensed, Taylor wanted to be baptized, at 15 years old and I got baptized again with her. Hallelujah!

  On November 19, 2013 (day after Taylor's 18th birthday), I was taken by ambulance from work because my supervisor thought I was having a heartache. The paramedics checked my blood pressure was like 200/110. I was in excruciating pain, and tears were flowing with my chest extremely tight! I got to St. Joseph's Hospital and taken straight back because they called me in as heart attack patient. I had every test run...Cat scan, EKG MRI, bloodwork, urine, etc. My daughter was called by my friend and supervisor to meet me at the hospital. She drove herself there calmly she added, and we were there for hours. The nurse (older White lady) came in and said, baby you need to be thanking God because every test came back negative! You had an anxiety attack and whatever is causing you that much stress, you need to let it go! I said yes ma'am!

Taylor graduated from high school, May 2014. My dad was released from prison at 68 years old in July 2014 and turned 69 the same month. My little cousin that stayed with me while she was at USF was keeping me updated because she assisted me with his affairs. Well once he got to the half-way house, he had a guy call me to let me know that he was there and I asked the guy why he was calling me, he replied your pops asked me too, but he is right here.

My dad got on the phone and did not talk. Once the call ended, I cried in astonishment! I just could not understand this man and I did not go to see him at the half-way house either. Taylor was leaving for college in Miami and wanted to see her granddaddy before she left. I did not want to go see him and I had to pray, but for her…anything! He was staying in Newberry at his sister's old house that was occupied by her children because she is deceased. He had his personal things mailed to me over the years to keep for him. I got his box of things and took them with us. We arrived and went in the house and he came out in a wheelchair in which he had been in a couple years due to his sciatic nerve issues. We spoke and I put his box down for him, while he was looking through it, I tried to have a conversation with him...nothing! Although he talked to Taylor a little bit. I told him that I thank God that he was free, and he replied, I have always been free! I said yes you have, but God answered my prayers to allow you to live long enough to be on the outside of those prison walls.

  My cousins were there quiet but observing the interaction between us and it was so awkward to say the least. I just could not wrap my head around what was his issue. After about 2 ½ hours, I was ready to go and I gave him a kiss on his forehead, and said I love you! Taylor said her goodbyes and they kissed, and we hit the road to Orlando. I was over it and him and cried! I was the best gift in his life, and he treated me like shit! A whole fucking joke!

  In August 2014, I took Taylor to Miami, and it was another emotional time for me because my baby was off to college. I had become an empty nester and I was so sad, for the first time since 1995, I was alone. I experienced separation anxiety pretty bad because she had become my sister/friend. Lord have mercy! I had to learn how to be alone all over again. I went to Miami every chance I got, which was frequently. I had bought Taylor a 2001 Mazda 626 from the auction through a coworker at Humana, the summer before her going into the 11th grade. However, my Saturn had died on me after 11 years and I had to start sharing my daughter's car therefore she had to go off to school without a vehicle.

In October 2014, my dad called me one day while at work upset because he was sick. He was turned down for Medicare and Medicaid. He would be approved for Medicare the following year, July 2015 at 70 years old, due to being incarcerated. I told him that I sold Medicare plans for a living with Humana, and he would be approved for Medicaid soon, but until then to go to the hospital for medical care. The hospital will not turn you away even without health insurance. He felt like he had the FLU and I told him to get checked out because it could develop into pneumonia, he started crying. This was the 3rd time my dad had cried to me in my lifetime.

I was pleading with him to explain to me what was going on? He would not respond. I was late returning from my break to get back on the phone and told him that I would call him back when I got off from work. I was alarmed because my dad was tough as nails and for him to cry…spoke volumes that something was terribly wrong!

On Friday, October 31, 2014, I was a football game in Lakeland (Kathleen High School and Lake Wales High School) with my litte sis D from work who was from Lakeland, and my cousin called me and said they had to call the ambulance to take my dad to the hospital and they would keep me posted. I started praying and left the game!

My dad was in the hospital a few days then moved to a rehab center. Once at the rehab center a nurse realized that his vitals were not strong enough to be there and he was taken back to the hospital by ambulance. I was being updated by my cousins on everything.

On Thursday, November 6, 2014, I received a call that the doctors were asking for the next of kin. I got up and packed my clothes and hit the road to Gainesville. I did not call my job or anyone…I was out! I prayed the whole drive there and asked God to prepare me, give me clarity and speak to me about what to do. I needed to know what was ahead of me. God spoke… it was bad and my dad was ready to go and he did not want to suffer, just like that! I went straight to the hospital and he was hooked up to all the machines. I spoke out loud and told my dad I was there and started praying aloud. My cousin came and stayed awhile with me. I called my daughter and she made it there from Miami. Every day, we went to the hospital from morning to evening, talking to the doctors, my cousins were in and out and I was praying each day but there was no improvement.

On Wednesday, November 12, 2014, I spoke to the doctor and asked if he thought there would be any change? He replied, I doubt it and I asked can I make the decision to take him off life support? The fluid on his lungs was not getting any better and his oxygen was declining each day. The doctor said yes, but he needed another doctor to agree with his decision. I said okay, let me wait until tomorrow. I called my cousin to contact all the family because God had given me the okay to take my dad off life support and we needed to all be present, to pray and say our last goodbyes. My heart was breaking but my spirit was strong because the Holy Spirit had prepared me on my drive from Tampa to Gainesville. I knew that my dad did not want to suffer any longer and it was time.

On Thursday, November 13, 2014, the next morning, I arrived at the hospital and the doctors came in and said they agreed, he was not going to improve. I said thank you for telling me and I needed some time. He said yes ma'am, just let me know when. I made the call…everyone came! We greeted one another, each took a turn talking to my dad, with my daughter never leaving his bedside. We prayed and sang aloud! Once the Holy Spirit gave me the okay, I called the doctor and gave him the word. He sent a nurse in to disconnect all the machines. I stayed by my dad's head praying and speaking life into his Spirit and I told him that I always loved him, but God loved him more and I kissed his forehead. My dad's heart stopped beating approximately 45 minutes after disconnecting him and everyone cried at different times and some left the room, but I stayed strong. Once he expired, I had to call his counselor at the half-way house. When he got there, he was so nervous and emotional, he also cried. He said, he never had an inmate to pass on his watch. He told me that my dad was very well liked and received by all the guys, and they called him pops. My dad had a perfect record during his incarceration, just as he did in the military as a soldier. He took all the information he needed from me and said that he would contact me back about funeral arrangements. When he left, I BROKE DOWN!

Not only so, but we also glory in our sufferings because we know that sufferings produces perseverance; perseverance, character; and character hope. And hope does not put us to shame, because God's love has been poured out into our hearts through the Holy Spirit, who has been given to us. Romans 5:3-5 (NIV)

We all left in a daze and met up for lunch at Red Lobster. I received a call that The Department of Corrections would pay for the funeral arrangements and I said no funeral just cremation, he said okay give me a funeral home. My cousins did the research for that and gave a local place. My daughter was DEVASTATED! My dad's baby sister which I had heard of in my 30's and only met recently said that I came there to kill her brother. Later went on to post ill things on Facebook, not the place! I went off in her IM! I literally wanted to fight her! The devil will use anyone, and he tried to use my anger to sniff me out! Bye Satan! This is the challenging part for me, older saints, saved people think they know everything! If you don't believe the Holy Spirit in someone, please go into your prayer closet and seek God to show you, by fasting and praying! I have done whatever God has instructed me to do regarding my immediate family and I am at peace with all my commitments to them! My cousins did everything they could for us while we were in Newberry/Gainesville because it was a very difficult time!

On Saturday, November 15, 2014, my little cousin got us tickets for The University of Florida and South Carolina game, at home in the Swamp. The game went into overtime and our Gators lost by 1 point. It was an intense game and my daughter, and I needed that excitement! It was her first time going to a college football game.

Fun, Fun, Fun!

We went to church and dinner with the family the next day then Taylor and I went back home to Tampa. I had been out on

FMLA for a week then bereavement for a week. My daughter contacted the school and her professors gave her time off from her classes due to the passing of her granddaddy.

On Tuesday, November 18, 2014 was Taylor's 19th birthday. I returned to work and on the first day back and I fell completely apart! I packed up my desk to quit and one of my day 1's saw me, and he walked with me to my car carrying my box. When he went back in the building, he told a supervisor which was a dear friend, and she called me and told me to go out on STD. I called the EAP line and found the most amazing therapist that I ever had to date. She was an older Middle Eastern women LCSW and Christian, her expertise was in trauma, sexual abuse, Domestic Violence, and sex trafficking. She helped put all the pieces of the puzzle together along with the Holy Spirit. She would have me explain events in 3rd person as if I was watching a movie. She went on to explain to me that I had never grieved my mom and my brother's death. My dad dying was the nail in the coffin because I had to relive each of their deaths and grieve properly. She said, I was sad and relieved because I no longer had the burden of taking care of everyone because all of them took a toll on my very existence.

After being on leave for 2 months, I returned to work January 2015. When I got back to work, I sat with other agents to do side-by-sides for 3 days before getting back on the phone. One day, my supervisor came running over to me asking me where I was because WFM was looking for me because I was not on the phone and I let her have it! I said, you approved for me to sit with someone and I am right on the same row as my desk, so why would you not explain to them where I was? She was looking at me like deer in the headlights. One thing for sure, I do not lie, and I will not tolerate anyone making me look like a liar! She said, I am going to get a manager. I said, you can go get anybody you want too, and I will tell them the same thing! When the manager called me in the office with her, I told him the same and his face turned red. I was back 3 weeks and I could not do it anymore and we mutually agreed that I would leave Humana after 7 years and 3 months. The stress was unbearable, and I needed peace. I would pull into the parking lot and would literally feel sick to my stomach to the point of vomiting. I kept in mind what that nurse said to me. I took a 6-month break from working and I started going to school in February 2015, after a 10-year break.

In August 2015, I had to get another vehicle because the transmission went out in my daughter's car. I got a 2013 Hyundai Elantra (2 years old, 1 owner, low miles) and I was excited to have a new whip!

I had a friend that I had known for 10 years that I met at AFS and I got her on at Humana, who had been asking me for about a year to be her roommate because she was having some financial issues. I was going through separation anxiety from my daughter being off to college, when Taylor finished her Freshman year I moved out of our place. I had been in a 2/2 apartment for nothing, at this point she was loving Miami. I ended up staying with the roommate for only 5 months because she was spending my money that I gave her for bills and the bills were coming back with disconnect notices in the mail.

One day, I told her that I would beat her ass about my money because I am responsible, and I pay my bills on time.

In January 2016, I moved into a 1/1 apartment close by my job (in the USF area). I lived there less than 30 days because I heard a shooting outside, maybe 50 yards from my front door and I experienced the worst PTSD after the incident because it triggered my mom's death. I was awakened from my sleep. I could not eat, sleep, have a bowel movement and I was nervous and paranoid for a couple months afterwards.

I also had to withdraw from my class at the time. The leasing office released me from my lease, without penalties, after getting my friend, who is a lawyer and my therapist involved, by showing documentation to solidify my case.

February 2016, I moved into another 1/1 apartment in Carrollwood, a much nicer area, working and going to school after work 6:00pm to 9:00pm twice a week. Everything was seemingly going well...then all hell broke out!

Conclusion

As I conclude my autobiography, I would like to express how grateful and humbled I am to share the most intimate parts of my life with the world. We live in a time of social media and great scrutiny, however God spoke to me and said for me to be okay with who I am. He made us all different and with His unique gifting's and plans in mind. Today when I look at myself in the mirror, I can smile because I now love the person I have become. I see a woman in the mirror that is an overcomer, fighter, and prayer warrior. I accept my flaws and weaknesses because they do not define me. God has kept me, and He has kept you if you are reading this book. He is not done with you! He is not done with you! He is not done with you! There is so much more to your story to be written in this journey called life!

But seek first the kingdom of God and His righteousness, and all these things shall be added to you. Therefore, do not worry about tomorrow, for tomorrow will worry about its own things. Sufficient for the day is its own trouble.
Matthew 6:33-34 (NKJV)

And I will restore to you the years that the locust hath eaten, the cankerworm, and the caterpillar, and the palmerworm, my great army which I sent among you. And ye shall eat in plenty, and be satisfied, and praise the name of the Lord your God that hath dealt wondrously with you: and my people shall never be ashamed. Joel 2:25-26 (KJV)

To everything there is a season, a time for every purpose under heaven: a time to be born, and a time to die; a time to plant, and a time to uproot what is planted; a time to kill, and a time to heal; a time to breakdown, and a time to build up; a time to weep, and a time to laugh; a time to mourn, and a time to dance; a time to cast away stones, and a time to gather stones; a time to refrain from embracing; a time to gain, and a time to lose; a time to keep, and a time to cast away; a time to tear, and a time to sew; a time to keep silence, and a time to speak; a time to love, and a time to hate; a time to war, and a time of peace. Ecclesiastes 3:1-8 (MEV)

"Goodbyes are only for those who love with their eyes. Because for those who love with heart and soul there is no such thing as separation."
-Rumi

In Loving Memory

Lorene Johnson Meeks December 2, 1949 to February 13, 1990 (mother)

Damon Demarcus Meeks July 13, 1980 to November 24, 1998 (brother)

Willie Meeks, Jr. July 12, 1945 to November 13, 2014 (father)

About the Author

I am the daughter of Lorene Meeks and Willie Meeks, Jr. I am a Florida Native. The oldest of two, a younger brother Damon Meeks my ace. My dad was in the military therefore I grew up as a military kid. I have lived in Florida, Germany, and Texas.

I have traveled all over the US, Germany, Italy, and Austria. The core values my parents instilled in me are independence, discipline, integrity, and compassion.

I am the mother to Taylor Wynn, my love and the grandmother to Tyler Brantley, my heart. I grew up going to church and loving God from 5 years old. I am a licensed Minister walking in several offices, prayer warrior, mentor, and exhorter.

My hope is that my testimony will encourage anyone who deals with anger and rage, depression, suicide, abandonment, displacement, and rejection to be overcomers, by following Jesus Christ.

Author's Contact Information:
Website: Officialrawrealrelatable.org
Instagram: rawrealrelatable
Twitter: rawrealrelatabl (No E)
Facebook: Dana Delores Meeks